Make a PACT for Success

Designing Effective Information Presentations

Ruth V. Small
Marilyn P. Arnone

The Scarecrow Press, Inc.
Lanham, Maryland, and London
2002

SCARECROW PRESS, INC.

Published in the United States of America
by Scarecrow Press, Inc.
A Member of the Rowman & Littlefield Publishing Group
4720 Boston Way, Lanham, Maryland 20706
www.scarecrowpress.com

4 Pleydell Gardens, Folkestone
Kent CT20 2DN, England

British Library Cataloguing in Publication Information Available

Library of Congress Cataloging-in-Publication Data

Small, Ruth V.
  Make a PACT for success : designing effective information presentations / Ruth V. Small, Marilyn P. Arnone.
    p. cm.
  Includes bibliographical references.
  ISBN 0-8108-4347-1 (pbk. : alk. paper)
    1. Public speaking. I. Arnone, Marilyn P. II. Title.
  PN4129.15 .S63 2002
    808.5'1—dc21   2002022373

♾™ The paper used in this publication meets the minimum requirements of American National Standard for Information Sciences—Permanence of Paper for Printed Library Materials, ANSI/NISO Z39.48-1992.
Manufactured in the United States of America.

Contents

Preface

The ability to effectively present information is a requirement in today's society. Once, merely taking a public speaking course in high school or college provided the skills needed to be an effective information presenter. However, with the explosive growth of information and information resources, information presentations are delivered not only through speech but also through electronic communications, audio and video media, and print materials. Each of those media has a range of formats, from newsletters to videos to live Webcasts, with common features as well as a number of unique delivery attributes that require individual consideration.

Most books on the topic of information presentations focus on the presentation delivery. Yet, to succeed in today's professional world, students must understand the characteristics of information and information need, understanding how to research, select, organize, and deliver information.

This book introduces the reader to three very important models that we believe are essential for the successful design, development, delivery, and evaluation of information presentations. The first is our PACT Model which provides a structure for thinking about a presentation, from determining its purpose and analyzing the potential audience to researching, organizing, and selecting content and identifying the most effective technique(s) for delivery. The second model is Taylor's Value-Added Processes, which pinpoints a number of attributes (e.g., currency, noise reduction, time-savings) that add value to the information used. The third is Keller's ARCS Model that prescribes a variety of motivational strategies for stimulating attention, providing relevance, and creating a presentation environment for the audience that ensures confidence and satisfaction with the experience.

Because this book integrates the critical information perspective for a range of information reporting and presentation modalities relevant to the professional arena, we expect it will be used in presentation skills courses offered in a variety of academic disciplines, such as management, public communications, speech communications, information studies, and writing. We also believe it is useful for individuals who are looking for a book that they can use on their own to help them develop presentation skills for work and for life.

Acknowledgments

The development of this book (our information presentation) was truly a team effort, requiring the input of many people. First, we wish to acknowledge John Keller and Bob Taylor, mentors, colleagues, and friends, whose work provided much of the inspiration behind this book and Pattee Fletcher for her valuable input early on in this project. We thank the faculty and students in the School of Information Studies at Syracuse University who formatively evaluated drafts of this book and provided invaluable feedback for improvement. We also wish to thank Alice Colasanti, Dr. Jacqueline Belen, Leni Binder, Donna Callahan, Joe Cox, Tom Hardy, Jill Hurst, Wayne Miner, and Kerry Ryan, nine very busy people, for giving generously of their time by sharing their presentation experiences with us. We gratefully acknowledge Beth Mahoney for her cheerful and expert assistance in the preparation of this manuscript and ArtToday (www.arttoday.com) for allowing us to use several of the graphics that appear within. Finally, we would like to thank our families for their support and encouragement throughout this long and arduous process.

Chapter 1

Getting Started

> *Information transfer is an intensely human process.*
>
> Robert S. Taylor, p. 1

In today's information-rich world, it is becoming increasingly imperative to acquire skills in the presenting and reporting of relevant, clear, concise information. To succeed in the professional world, however, you need more than simply skills for *delivering* presentations. One must also understand the characteristics of information, information need, and information use. The increasing popularity of electronic information resources such as online databases and the Internet, while providing a wealth of information, adds to the necessity of having an "information toolbox" to sort through and use information in a range of professional settings.

You are about to discover a proven way, the PACT Model for Designing Effective Information Presentations[©], to develop just such a toolbox in order to increase your skills in preparing and delivering winning business presentations in a variety of formats. We use the word "presentation" in a generic sense throughout this book, meaning anything from a live presentation to a written report to multimedia or some combination.

Consider this book as your "training program" for developing the skills mentioned above. All other skills being equal, expertise in the presentation of information will set you apart in the professional world and may even be the deciding factor for being hired and promoted. Your training goal is to acquire the knowledge and master the skills that will make you such an expert. Just like athletic training, confidence is key and practice makes perfect.

We have interspersed a variety of exercises and activities throughout this book to help you hone those skills, as well as a running case study to offer opportunities for reflection and the generation of new ideas. We'll do our best to motivate you along the way. So read on and be sure to practice your newly developed skills. You'll find the rewards well worth the effort!

Objectives

By the end of chapter 1, you should be able to:

- describe in a general way what the acronym PACT means, and
- identify the components of presentation design and development.

An Overview of the Model

PACT is an acronym for the following four essential components of any presentation. They are:

Purpose (Why?)
Audience (Who?)
Content (What?)
Technique (How?)

If you attend to all of these components, you will have created your own PACT for presentation success. In chapter 2, we'll begin to explore each of the components in detail but, for now, we would like to simply introduce you to the model.

Where do you start? PACT is not a purely step-by-step model but rather an iterative one in which you must clearly understand the purpose of the presentation *and* your audience *before* you can begin to think about what content you will teach and technique(s) you will use to deliver that content. We use the word "audience" broadly to represent those people who receive your presentation. Audience could mean members of a live audience, readers of your written report, viewers/users of your multimedia Web site, etc. Often, you have to rethink your purpose once you have identified your audience and determined your content and technique, thus the iterative nature of the model. Likewise, the content you include and the technique you choose will be highly influenced by your purpose and what you know about your audience. This interdependence of the four PACT components is illustrated in the graphic on the following page.

PACT Model©

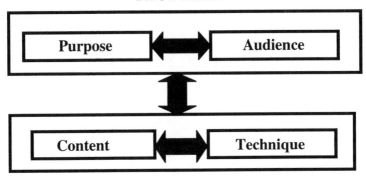

Let's begin with a hypothetical scenario. Suppose you are the Information Technology (IT) Coordinator for a local nonprofit agency. The Executive Director asks you to develop and present the agency's new IT policy to its sixteen employees. She has allocated a portion of the next staff meeting for you to do so.

Now let's think of your task in terms of the PACT Model. It's always tempting to skip right to the content or technique before considering your purpose and audience. This can cause serious problems down the road. For example, if you design a presentation to inform your audience but you really need to influence their opinions, your presentation could have little or no effect. If you prepare a presentation for a mixed audience and then discover you have an audience of experts, it is likely that your presentation will bore your audience.

As you begin to define the purpose of your presentation, you first must establish whether there is truly a need for a formal presentation. Ask yourself, "What do I want my audience to do or feel as a result of my presentation?" Then, from a *planning* perspective, learn everything you can about the situation in which you will be presenting—things like the size of the room, time of day, number of people comprising your audience, availability of technology, etc., since all of these factors will affect how (and how well) you present your information. Remember, a presentation can take a number of forms, from a written report to an oral presentation to a single medium or multimedia presentation (or some combination of these), and planning becomes a critical part of the entire design and development process from beginning to end. We describe purpose in the next chapter.

Once you have determined the purpose of your presentation, you should turn your attention to learning as much as you can about your audience (*who* are they?). We call this an "audience analysis" and you'll find out what's involved in an audience analysis in chapter 3. In our scenario, you may already know a great deal about your audience since you all work for the same organization. Do you think your audience will be favorable toward implementing a new IT policy? Do you believe there will be some resistance? How much does your audience already know about the new policy? These are just some of the questions you need to answer concerning your audience. You will learn more about audience analysis in chapter 3.

You'll also need to know what and how much content to select and how to organize your presentation. What information will you present? Should you begin with an overview of the entire new IT policy or with key parts? How much information is needed? Will you need to incorporate additional examples to help clarify the more abstract content? There are different ways to organize the content in your presentation based on its purpose. Organization, amount, and type of information are all important factors to consider for the content aspect of PACT. We provide answers to these questions (and more) in chapters 4, 5, and 6.

Finally, technique focuses on the "how tos" of developing effective presentations. It includes such things as personal presentation skills, format, and media selection and use. Some questions you might want to answer related to technique are: How can I effectively present my content to my audience? How can I use media effectively? How will I overcome anxiety? We discuss various techniques in chapters 7, 8, and 9.

You will also eventually want to examine the effectiveness and efficiency of your final presentation. You might want to ask questions such as: How will I know that my presentation was effective? How can I improve it for the next time? Evaluation is a critical part of any presentation, not only after it is completed but also at critical points along the way. We discuss evaluation in more detail in chapter 10.

Presentation Design and Development Issues

Purpose and audience comprise the *design* phase of creating a presentation while content and technique are the primary factors in the *development* phase of information presentation design. Identifying your presentation's purpose and gathering as much information as possible about your audience provide you with essential information for selecting and organizing your content and determining the technique(s) you will use to deliver that content.

Although the PACT Model may seem like a linear process, it is not lockstep. Establishing the purpose and audience are the necessary first things to be considered. Think of this as a "blueprint," much like the type that architects create. A blueprint must be created to provide the specifications for actually building the structure. Consider what could happen if the architect just went right to the building stage and skipped the blueprint process. Now, consider the same thing if you ignore your purpose and audience and begin with your content and technique.

In the development phase, it is not uncommon to work in teams, where one person works on content while another focuses on some aspect of technique. You may also need to rethink some aspects of your purpose and audience as you proceed through the development phase, especially when someone else has determined either or both of these dimensions. For example, a market researcher may have collected data on the target audience for the new company Web site you are developing. This information provides new insights as you reconsider the specifications of your presentation. This type of iterative process, in which you revisit some previous step either for clarification or modification, is the norm in presentation creation.

Organizational Identity

One of the first tasks of any newly formed organization is determining its mission and goals, scope, target audience, specific products and/or services, etc. This is called an *organizational identity*.

Writing your organizational identity is just that—identifying the critical aspects of your organization including what makes it unique and marketable. But it is even more. It is creating the *image* you wish your organization to present to the public. For example, what might your organization's logo look like and how will it translate to a letterhead, business card, brochure, report, etc.? Does your organization have a slogan? Will it be a phrase, a simple statement, humorous or serious? Unless you are a graphic artist, most likely you will never have to actually design and execute the logo or artistic product. Once your organizational identity is established, it will form the basis of any presentations you do for your organization.

This Book: What It Is and What It Isn't

This book presents a new and different way to look at presentations *from an information perspective*. Therefore, the book is not about how to technically put together a PowerPoint presentation or how to become a whiz at using desktop publishing software. It is not a primer on public speaking or on technical writing. There are other books that do a fine job at that (several of which are referenced in this book).

As you read this book, you will discover that, while all of those formats are discussed (and even focused on) at various times, it takes a broader approach, focusing on the *information* aspects of presentations, that is, the process of defining, selecting, organizing, managing, presenting, and evaluating information to communicate a message to a given audience.

To succeed in today's professional world, you must have an understanding of the characteristics of information, information need, and information use regardless of the presentation format or medium. You must understand how to clearly and concisely present information tailored for a specific need and often targeted to a specific audience. As you proceed through this book, you will have opportunities to sharpen your personal presentation skills and you will soon discover that those skills will become stronger and stronger as you build confidence in your ability to work with information in various presentation modes.

We begin each chapter with a relevant *hook* to capture your attention (e.g., a graphic, a quote) and alert you to what content will be covered in that chapter. Throughout the book we have sprinkled real-life anecdotes that exemplify concepts presented. We have also made this book an interactive presentation, providing "Flashbacks" and posing questions and situations for you to "Think About" at various points in each chapter.

At the end of every chapter, we include our ongoing case study where you can follow the progress and activities of the managers of our fledgling company, Digital Denim, Inc. (DD Inc.). We introduce DD Inc. at the end of this chapter and focus on a different situation in which one of the managers finds himself or herself in each of the subsequent chapters. We hope the case study will stimulate your thinking and discussion. We use the case study as a way to exemplify specific dimensions of the PACT Model and to provide a basis for the end-of-chapter "Do & Discuss" section. "Do & Discuss" provides opportunities for individuals, small groups, or an entire class to reflect and apply the concepts presented. We also include a "Learning Check" at the end of each chapter that asks you questions about some of the key concepts covered in the chapter (the answers to which may be found in appendix A).

In every chapter, we also include a special feature called "Let's Hear It" in which we describe the results of interviews with real people from a wide variety of contexts, from medicine to government to IT training to entertainment, who share with you their memorable presentation experiences. We intersperse their accounts with our comments. We think you'll find yourself going back and rereading their stories as you learn more about the design and development of successful information presentations. Finally, "Coming Up ... " gives you a sneak preview of the succeeding chapter.

In our final chapter, we end with our *sinker*, an interactive way to conclude this book. We present five presentation scenarios that require you to apply many of the concepts presented in this book. This exercise also allows you the opportunity to discover how much you have learned about designing, developing, delivering, and evaluating effective information presentations.

Let's Hear It! ⁙⏝

The Director of Marketing for feature films at a major film studio in Los Angeles (we'll call her Joanna as she wishes to remain anonymous) was asked to make an influencing presentation for her company's home entertainment division that promotes home videos and DVDs. The audience was made up of 300-400 retailers (e.g., Target, Wal-Mart, Blockbuster) who carry the product for rental or sale to consumers. The presentation was given on the stage of the auditorium in the John F. Kennedy Center in Washington, D.C., a somewhat intimidating venue for anyone.

Joanna faced several other major challenges with her presentation. "Our presentation was at about three o'clock in the afternoon, after lunch, about the worst time possible," she moaned. Time of day can be a major factor in the success of a presentation. Mid-afternoon, after eating a meal, an audience can be very sleepy and inattentive.

But this wasn't the only challenge Joanna faced. "I shared our part of the presentation with a person who does a lot of research for our company." We would characterize his part of the presentation as the *informing* part of the duo. "We combined the research with how we promoted our overall media and promotional campaign, focusing on how we were going to promote home videos and DVDs to get retailers to buy it for their stores as well as our game plan to motivate consumers to actually go out and say 'I *have* to have that DVD as part of my collection!' My part of the presentation was approximately twenty minutes long." So Joanna had only twenty minutes to present her part of the presentation, which we characterize as *influencing*.

In addition, they shared the stage with some very impressive speakers. "We were on the same program with a well-known head of a major film production company and General Colin Powell (our current U.S. Secretary of State). I thought for sure I would be the 'muffin break-bathroom break,' " Joanna said with a laugh.

So, how did Joanna meet the challenges she faced? "The format of the presentation was a PowerPoint style but it was done on a large screen and we had incorporated video clips into it (movies, trailers, and stunts) and a lot of online stuff to illustrate various points we were making. After my partner presented the research, I had to present overall what our media campaign would be in order to get retailers excited about buying our product. We want them to buy hundreds of thousands of copies of things. In this case we wanted to promote a specific movie," she explained.

Joanna had to find a way to influence her audience to choose her product. That meant that her presentation had to be interesting, innovative, and memorable. "We had to consider what our competition was doing at the time. When you have any kind of product coming out, another studio is also releasing its product. You have two different titles and these retailers only have so much shelf space. If you only have enough room for a certain quantity, everybody is competing, saying 'Buy me! Buy me!' and the retailer has to make choices."

So Joanna had to come up with a creative presentation idea. "We tried to be very clever by spoofing the characters of our competitor's film. For example, in our movie there is a character that has sword-like fingers. Our competitor's movie (where the central characters were chickens) was coming out at the same time and it was around Thanksgiving, so we decided to turn a traditional Thanksgiving turkey carving scene into one in which their chicken was the one being carved," Joanna said with a smile.

"There was another character in our film who wore special goggles so we made lightning bolts coming out of his eyes that bombarded the main character of our competitor's fast-paced adventure film that was also being released for home viewing at that time. We also had another of our characters use the lightning bolts to hit the boat in another competitor's film about a storm disaster at sea. The idea was that our character had actually caused their 'perfect' storm, so retailers should buy *our* product." Joanna also provided her audience with a one-page handout containing several facts about their campaign, such as how many people they would reach and how much money they were putting behind their media campaign.

It sounded to us like Joanna's creative ideas were very costly and not within the reach of most presenters but she corrected our assumption. "Most of the presentation was done in PowerPoint and stills that we had. We used pieces of an existing trailer and other creative material from the Internet and elsewhere that we already owned and put it together in a way that it made it look like a full-fledged presentation."

What were the outcomes of Joanna's presentation? "The goal was to motivate retailers to buy our product for their stores and there are also consumer sales goals that are pre-set by our company. We exceeded all goals. In fact, consumers went out and actually made the purchases to such an extent that we were back ordered! We had to go back to press to print more videos and DVDs."

But Joanna's success wasn't limited to meeting company goals. It also meant a personal reward for Joanna. "As a result of my presentation," she said, "the company moved me from home entertainment to the theatrical group which was considered a promotion in itself because you're working on first-run releases."

When we asked Joanna what had been the main contributing factor that made her presentation a success, she responded, "It was the use of clever humor. It was the play on words. It was the images of the two titles competing against each other and we wanted to present that without being too focused on number-crunching. A lot of times when people compare things in any comparative analysis they talk about dollar figures, statistics, and how things did last year. That's all very important information but you have people at three o'clock in the afternoon and they're not going to listen and take that away. But they are going to remember our actress with lightning bolts around her and our competitor's boat tipping over, thinking we were responsible for creating this disaster. They thought it was cool and they wanted to see what was going to come next. It was nice to have a little laughter in the room by the end of the day."

The use of humorous imagery made Joanna's presentation memorable. "Visuals make such an impact but you have to be careful not to go overboard. If it's too much, they'll think it's overkill." This is great advice. Motivational strategies, like a little creative humor, can go a long way. Thinking of ways to present dry or potentially boring information in exciting ways will help make a good presentation great, just as Joanna's experience illustrates.

What Is Digital Denim, Inc.?

Digital Denim, Inc. is a company founded several years ago and headquartered in New York City. It was one of the first specialized clothing companies in the United States to use information technology in every aspect of its business. After establishing a presence in the fashion industry through its popular bricks-and-mortar stores in New York and Los Angeles where customers use computers to order items they want to their specifications, DD Inc. went beyond using the Internet simply for marketing and commerce tasks, developing innovative software to create an "electronic boutique" on the World Wide Web where consumers can design and customize their own denim clothing and accessories—all in the digital domain.

Customers may select color, texture, size, shape, or cut. They can even scan personal photos (which can be updated when appropriate) that are stored, so that each time they visit DD Inc. online, they can "try on" their items in the site's trendy electronic "fitting room" before making a decision about a purchase.

Consumers can also choose to interact with well-known clothing designers who will invite them into their virtual showrooms. Here, the designers provide fashion tips and advice based on customer input. They even offer the consumer the opportunity to participate in their virtual fashion shows! DD Inc. online offers unique products and services not available at its retail stores, promoting them through a variety of media such as fashion magazines, billboards, television, brochures, and the Web.

Learning Check

1.   What are the four components of the PACT Model?

2. Which are considered the "design" components and which are the "development" components of PACT?

3. What is some of the information that makes up an organizational identity?

Do & Discuss

Join forces with three or four classmates and form a hypothetical company that is initiating an Internet presence. The company's products or services may be an improved-upon version of other existing products or services or may be something brand-new or futuristic. Some examples are a new type of database travel service and a "touch" menu that automatically translates a restaurant's menu item to a language of choice. Feel free to be creative.

*   Create an organizational identity for your company by answering the following questions:
    *   Who are we?
    *   What is our mission?
    *   What do we sell?
    *   Who are our customers?
    *   Who is our competition?
    *   What is unique about our company?
    *   How do we use information technology in our business?

*   Briefly describe the location (if there is one), size of your business, length of time in business, information about your industry in general, and any other information you think is important.

*   After you have completed the above, get creative and develop a logo and slogan for your company that represents your corporate image.

In chapter 2 we'll focus on the most important step for getting off to a good start in whatever presentation you undertake: gaining a thorough understanding of your presentation's purpose.

Source of Quote

Taylor, Robert S. (1986). *Value-Added Processes in Information Systems*. Norwood, N.J.: Ablex Publishing Corporation, p. 1.

Chapter 2

P Is for Purpose

PACT Model©

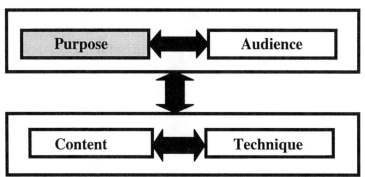

Let's begin by returning to our little scenario in chapter 1, the one where you are the IT Coordinator in a small non-profit agency. Your boss has asked you to present the new IT policy to employees at the next staff meeting.

As soon as you get your knees to stop shaking, what's the first thing you need to do? (Quitting your job is not an option.) After taking a calming breath or two, your first task is to make sure you understand clearly the purpose of the presentation. It may seem clear-cut or, as they used to say in the old *Dragnet* television show, "Just the facts, ma'am." That is what we call a simple informing presentation. But is it?

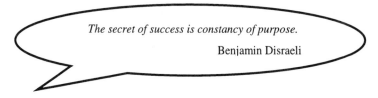

The secret of success is constancy of purpose.

Benjamin Disraeli

In this chapter, we'll explore several presentation purposes. Once you have nailed your purpose, you can do some preliminary *planning* (so you might say that P is also for *planning*). We will discuss both of these important aspects of the *design* phase.

Objectives

By the end of chapter 2, you should be able to:

- define four purposes for presentations,
- identify several situational variables for which you must prepare,
- describe the rationale for thinking of yourself as a presentation project manager, and
- identify some of the responsibilities of a presentation project manager.

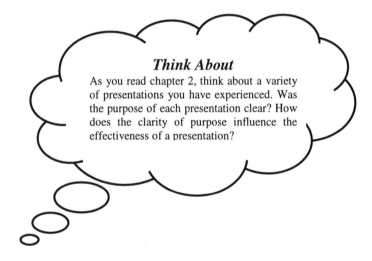

Think About

As you read chapter 2, think about a variety of presentations you have experienced. Was the purpose of each presentation clear? How does the clarity of purpose influence the effectiveness of a presentation?

The "Is" Have It!

There are four main purposes for information presentation. To make them easier to remember, we'll call them the four "Is." They are:

- Informing
- Inspiring
- Influencing
- Instructing

They represent the overarching goal of your presentation; you will naturally have specific objectives subsumed under your broad goal (which we discuss later). Let's begin by examining the four Is in more detail.

The Informing Presentation

When your purpose is simply *to inform* your audience, you are concerned with presenting the facts, explaining a situation, presenting a new concept, or making your audience aware of something new. You could also call it the "explanation" presentation, since your main goal is to explain something. Informing presentations do not usually include recommendations; they are simply intended to present the facts. Some examples of an informing presentation are:

- an organization's annual report
- a company's organizational chart
- a sign giving directions to various locations within the company's facility

Another example would be introducing employees to an organization's new IT policy. "Ah-ha!" you say, that is just the type of presentation introduced in our scenario in which you were assigned to present the agency's new IT policy. Thus, it must be an informative presentation. That would be an accurate assumption. Yet, there may be more to it than that, so read on.

The Inspiring Presentation

The purpose of an inspiring presentation is to stimulate an emotional response in your audience. You could also call this type of presentation a "motivational" presentation. Here's an example. Shoe sales at the local department store are up 25 percent over the same quarter of the previous year. The manager feels she can do even better next quarter. She rounds up the employees of the shoe department for a recognition breakfast, presents her top performers with plaques for outstanding performance, praises the department overall, and proceeds to give them a pep talk anticipating great success in the next quarter and emphasizing how their success has an impact on the entire company.

The purpose of the shoe department manager's presentation is *to inspire* or to motivate employees to exceed their previous performance. She uses several strategies to achieve this, including praise and external rewards. As long as she doesn't accidentally overlook anyone who should be recognized (when this happens, the result is de-motivation), and she is realistic about expectations for the next quarter, she will succeed in her overarching goal—to inspire employees.

Let's return to our chapter 1 scenario. As IT Coordinator, you have to present a new IT policy to the organization's employees. We have already agreed that the main purpose of your presentation would be to inform employees. But is there more? Perhaps. What if the policy could be perceived by some employees as threatening? Your job may also include motivating your audience and making them feel confident about the new policy. Therefore, you will need to identify benefits of the new policy that might offset any negativity from employees. This is an example of a presentation where the primary purpose would be to inform but a secondary purpose would be to inspire.

As you read this last paragraph, you may have been thinking, "Uh oh! I guess I will have to have some information about the people who will comprise my audience in order to accurately define my purpose." You're absolutely right! But put that thought on hold temporarily. We'll talk more about analyzing your audience in chapter 3.

> *What an audience thinks of a persuader may be directly influenced by what they think of his message.*
>
> Marvin Karlins & Herbert I. Abelson, p. 122

The Influencing Presentation

This type of presentation is called the *influencing presentation* because your job is to influence your audience so that (1) they can make a certain decision or (2) you can change their minds about an issue. You may notice that there are aspects of the inspiring presentation here as well. However, your presentation must go beyond inspiring, since your goal is for your audience to ultimately make a choice resulting in some action on their part and your goal is to influence that choice.

There are other ways of describing this type of presentation. You may hear it referred to as a *persuasional* presentation or an *advocacy* presentation.[1] The main purpose, however, is to persuade or influence your audience to take a particular point of view.

Since you will also need to include at least some facts to support your argument, there are necessarily aspects of an informing presentation as well. Marketing and sales presentations generally include aspects of all three types of presentation discussed so far, with their *primary* function being to convince the audience to purchase a product or service.

The influencing presentation is by far the most challenging and encompassing. Why is this type of presentation so challenging? It is because there are many audience factors to consider. For example, your audience may already have preconceived notions about your intention, or they may already hold a strong opinion on the issues you plan to discuss. The place and time of day will also have an effect on their attitudes about and their attention to your presentation.

Flashback

Remember Joanna's presentation described in the "Let's Hear It!" in chapter 1? Place and time of day were definitely challenges to her presentation success. How your audience perceives you (as the creator, and possibly deliverer, of the presentation) will also affect whether you have a chance of bringing them around to your point of view. All of these variables will be addressed in more detail in chapter 3.

The Instructing Presentation

Your overall purpose in an instructing presentation is for your audience to learn something new (to them) such as a new skill or procedure or perhaps to understand a new concept. It is different from the informing presentation because the instructing presentation goes beyond simply *presenting* information. This type of presentation may also include providing your audience with opportunities to practice or apply the newly learned information. Occasionally, your audience will have to demonstrate knowledge and skills through some sort of testing. As an instructing presenter, you may have to prepare materials for your audiences that will help them learn effectively and efficiently. We think of this book as primarily an instructing presentation because its goal is for you to learn how to design effective information presentations and we include practice opportunities through exercises and activities to help you do that.

In the business world, the instructing presentation is often delivered as a training session or program, i.e., one instructional session among many. While employee training is an important function of business, the instructing presentation is more likely to be delivered by individuals whose job descriptions are narrowly defined as *trainers*. However, there are times (particularly when dealing with information technology) when managers have to teach something to someone. For example, you might have to train new staff or interns. Or, you may have to teach your co-workers (or even your boss) a new skill learned at a professional workshop or conference. You will almost always have to reinforce their newly learned skills as they're performing their job. One common type of instructing presentation for accomplishing this is the *job aid*. Job aids are one of the few types of instructing presentation we'll discuss in this book (see chapter 7).

After establishing the overall purpose of your project, you will need to define some of the more specific objectives. In the department store example mentioned earlier, we established that the major purpose of the manager's presentation was to inspire her employees to achieve even greater sales in the upcoming quarter. From that overarching purpose, the manager would have to define some specific *measurable* objectives in order to know if that goal had been achieved. For example, her objectives might include:

- The department will increase sales of casual shoes by 15 percent.
- The department will increase sales of career shoes by 12 percent.
- Employees will demonstrate a positive attitude toward achieving higher sales.

Based on her specific objectives, the shoe department manager would organize the information to be presented (the *content* aspect of PACT) in such a way as to achieve these objectives; that is, the desired motivational effect and subsequent increase in sales.

Finding out whether a presentation's goals and objectives have been met is accomplished through some type of evaluation effort. Evaluating the effectiveness of a presentation will be thoroughly discussed in chapter 10. However, evaluating your purpose and how to achieve it is something you need to start thinking about during the presentation design stage.

P also Stands for Planning

As we mentioned earlier in this chapter, planning is also a critical part of the design phase of presentation creation. You might want to begin by mentally putting yourself in the place of your audience and answering the following question: What would *I* want to get out of this presentation?

Once you have answered this question, there are two aspects of planning to be considered:

1. identifying the specifics of the presentation situation, and
2. managing your overall project (creating the presentation).

Identifying the Specifics of the Presentation Situation

This aspect of presentation design is relatively easy to do but also can be quite tedious. However, it is a critical step because understanding the situation will help guide most of the decisions you make concerning your presentation. For example, if you know your presentation will be at the end of a long workday, you would want to be sensitive to a potentially tired audience—one that would be highly appreciative if your presentation were short and sweet.

Timing could also apply to a written report. Let's assume your boss only has a brief time to read your report before heading off to use the information in a meeting out of state. How would you deal with that? One way is to construct a clear and concise *executive summary* (this topic is addressed in chapter 7) of the full report and provide some visuals (e.g., charts, graphs) for his quick review. You might also include pointers to more detailed information in the full report for quick and easy reference. He will appreciate the brevity of the executive summary while feeling confident that he can cite supporting facts and other detailed information, if necessary, quickly and easily during his meeting.

Aside from time of day, there are other factors in the presentation situation to consider such as location, size of room or presentation space (e.g., office, auditorium), number of anticipated attendees, and availability of technology. If you have to deliver an oral presentation in a large room, for instance, you have to consider the acoustics of the room to determine how sound will carry. You may need to check to make certain that provisions are made to amplify your voice.

If you are presenting certain visuals, you might also have to determine if the room can be (and must be) darkened. We know a case where a well-known expert on the subject of learning disabilities was asked to present the keynote address at a state conference of 200 special educators. She had developed a slide-tape presentation that demanded a darkened room. However, when she arrived at the conference center on that bright, sunny day, she discovered that the auditorium in which she was assigned to speak had ceiling-to-floor windows with no shades and a thirty-foot high ceiling. To her dismay, she realized that anyone beyond the third row of the auditorium would be unable to clearly see most of her presentation. What did she do? She had to verbally describe each slide as she proceeded through her prepared text so that the people sitting beyond the tenth row could understand her presentation. This added to the amount of time she needed to present and, since she had a prescribed time limit, she was unable to share all of the content she had prepared. Seeking information about the presentation environment during the design phase was a critical factor for the success of her presentation that, unfortunately, she failed to consider.

This example illustrates two critical rules of thumb for planning a presentation:
1.   Always do a *background check* of the presentation environment as part of your design activity.
2.   Always have a *back-up plan*!

Background Check

Another major situation variable that can have a major effect on the success of a presentation in today's world is technology. With the availability and relative ease of presentation software, anyone can create a highly professional-looking set of presentation slides with sound, animation, video and/or graphics.

Let's say you find out the place where you will deliver your oral presentation on the new IT policy has an excellent computer-based projection unit and large screen, a high-quality speaker system, and flexible lighting. You plan on using computer support, so you're all set, no need to worry about your technology support, right? Wrong! That's just when the worst can (and often does) happen. You might discover (typically at the last minute) that the facility does not have the right connectors for your particular computer or that for some unknown reason the system is down on the particular day of your presentation. There's no escape. You are facing your audience; your colleagues are blocking the exits. Your heart starts to race, and the perspiration beads on your forehead start to give you away. How could you have prevented this or at least have been prepared for the worst?

First of all, make sure to check the room out if at all possible ahead of time. Bring your computer and check that the connectors, cables, and all the other paraphernalia you plan to use are supported by the in-house system. If you cannot visit the location ahead of time (laziness is not an acceptable excuse; a presentation at a location that is thousands of miles away is), then clearly communicate your needs to the person at the presentation site who is responsible for your technology arrangements. Let him or her know exactly what equipment you are bringing and specifically what you will need. Then confirm the arrangements in a fax, letter, or email to that individual. Putting it in writing will increase its importance and the likelihood that things will be in order when you arrive on the big day.

Background checks may also be important for other types of presentations, as well. For example, if you are designing a Web site for use in K-12 education and plan to include several videos that require high bandwidth, you will want to make sure that your target audience (i.e., schools) have the needed bandwidth to accommodate your videos. If they do not, you have to consider whether (1) they might obtain the technology in the near future, (2) the videos are critical to the message, and (3) other ways to deliver the information, such as text descriptions or PowerPoint slides.

Back-Up Plan

Now, you can sit back and relax about such things and move on to the meat and potatoes of your presentation, right? Wrong again. Even if all or the above arrangements are taken care of, do not assume that things will go off without a hitch. When they do, it's a great feeling, but all too often there is an unexpected snag. Your job is to expect the unexpected and be prepared. From a technology perspective, that means: Always have a Plan B. What's your back-up if, for instance, your computer fails on the day of your presentation just as you finish testing it with the in-house system that incidentally worked beautifully until now? One means of back-up is to have a low-tech version (such as overhead transparencies) of your presentation content. In this case, asking for an overhead projector as a back-up system would be wise (and don't forget to bring extra bulbs). Chances are that both the in-house system and the overhead projector won't disappoint you at the very same time. However, you can never tell what might go wrong.

One of the authors was delivering a slide-tape presentation to an audience of about 100 people. Before her audience arrived, she rehearsed the presentation twice on the equipment and in the assigned room in which the presentation would be given just to be sure everything worked flawlessly. However, just as she began the actual presentation, the projector bulb blew! Anticipating this possibility, the presenter pulled a new bulb from her pocket. To her horror, she discovered that in order to replace the bulb, she needed a screwdriver to open the bulb compartment. Luckily for her, someone in the audience had a small pocket-sized screwdriver in his briefcase. From that moment on, the author carries a small screwdriver with her to all presentations. This story illustrates that you can never be overprepared for any presentation.

Some of us are not comfortable unless we have a backup for our back-up. If you are one of these folks, try to have a lower-tech alternative, for example a flip chart (if your audience is relatively small), handouts that outline key points in your oral presentation, or even a written report to replace a video or multimedia presentation that fails. If you really know your stuff, you will still do well in such situations. Although we will not be discussing content or specific techniques until later in this book, it is important to mention here that right from the very beginning, you must perform a background check of the presentation environment and have a back-up plan in order to maximize your chances of having a successful presentation.

Managing the Overall Presentation Project

Part of the planning process requires you to act as your presentation's project manager. You might be wondering why we use the term "project manager" when talking about presentations. After all, project management generally involves a team of persons assigned to different tasks on a project that is large in scope. Well, a presentation should be thought of as a project. Even if it only involves yourself (you are the only person responsible for planning the presentation, developing its content, selecting the delivery techniques), it is still a project in which you must manage many details.

Once you begin your project, you may discover that you do, in fact, need the input of others to complete your presentation (e.g., someone has relevant statistical information you need, another has old photographs you would like to incorporate, etc.). If your presentation is in the form of multimedia or a written report, it will likely require that you have others contributing to your project (both of these types of presentations will be explored later in this book).

Even if you are primarily working alone on a project, you may find it important to utilize as many relevant human and material resources as possible to do the best job possible. Sometimes the quality of your research can have a profound effect on the effectiveness of your presentation (we discuss this further in chapter 6). Remember this important point: If you do not or cannot delegate responsibility to someone with expertise in the required task whenever you have the opportunity, the outcome of your presentation or product is limited to what you, yourself, can do.

Now, let's discuss some of the nitty gritty elements with respect to you as a project manager. What do project managers do? Or, more to the point, what should you do as the project manager for your presentation? You'll need to address the following fundamental considerations.

Timeframe

How much lead time do you have before your report or presentation is due? Whether you have a short or long lead time, you will need to make decisions about how much can actually be accomplished given the time parameters. A couple of overused cliches come to mind: "Never bite off more than you can chew" and "Under-promise and over-deliver."

Budget

First of all, do you even *have* a budget? If you are planning to present a status report on a recent project to the directors of your company, chances are you have little or no budget with which to work. Most likely, you would not need much financial support to complete that type of presentation project.

On the other hand, if you have been commissioned to prepare a written prospectus on the new directions your company is taking to increase revenue for a group of potential investors, then you may be given a sizable budget. For this group, you might need some "bells and whistles," perhaps some multimedia, handouts, the works. What you need to remember is to establish your budget up front, so that you can allocate your funds wisely and you can then focus your efforts on creating a dynamite presentation.

Available Resources

As mentioned earlier, even if you are working with a non-existent budget, you may have other resources available to you. These might range from copy paper to report covers to a laptop computer. Use them.

Task Clarification

This book provides the PACT Model to use as a guide to the design and development aspects of your presentation. However, if you are utilizing any human resources for your project, it is necessary to explicitly define the tasks and the expected outcomes for whoever works with you. For example, if you need the creative input and services of the in-house graphic artist, make sure he or she understands the overall vision for your presentation and the timeframe for the needed services. It is best to confirm this in a memo (see chapter 7) to the individual (with a copy to his or her boss), to prevent the assignment from unintentionally slipping to the bottom of the pile.

Communication

If you are working alone on your presentation project, you may only need to communicate to your superior to ask a question or to report your progress, if that is expected. When working with a team, you need to communicate regularly, providing progress reports, occasional-to-frequent encouragement, and conflict resolution when necessary.

Project management is an important part of the planning aspect of the presentation design process and we have only touched on it here. Most important to remember, it is essential for you to assume the mentality of a project manager when designing presentations using the PACT Model. You will become more efficient and will increase your professionalism as an information presenter.

Let's Hear It!

Joseph H. Cox is Manager of Training Technologies at Shaw Industries, Inc. in Dalton, Georgia. Shaw Industries Inc., a subsidiary of Berkshire Hathaway Inc., is the largest manufacturer of carpet in the world. It is a geographically dispersed organization with one hundred facilities (manufacturing and distribution centers and sales offices) throughout the United States. The company sells its products directly to retailers (national and local stores, such as Sears).

In the past, the IT training department (consisting of Joe and three trainers) has confined itself to training employees to use a variety of desktop computer applications, such as Microsoft Office. Now, the department wants to expand its scope beyond what Joe refers to as "shrink-wrapped applications" and beyond their typical instructor-led, classroom-based training to develop a corporate-wide e-learning solution. While Joe and his staff had trained an impressive 3900+ employees at Shaw over the past year, they want to be able to reach an even greater number of Shaw employees across the country.

Joe developed an influencing presentation whose purpose was to seek approval from upper-level management at Shaw to proceed with the proposed corporate-wide e-learning program. His audience consisted of Shaw's Vice President, CIO, Director of Information Systems Planning, Director of Systems Development, and Director of Information Technology Services. The presentation took place in a conference room with everyone seated around a large table. (This arrangement facilitated the discussion that followed with everyone facing everyone else.) There was projection equipment and a large screen in the room. Joe was the sole presenter.

Was Joe nervous? Not on your life! Joe was fully prepared for the presentation he was about to deliver. First of all, he had piloted e-training sessions with eighty-five of Shaw's facilities nationwide. This provided excellent evidence of what could be accomplished with full implementation of Joe's proposed project. Secondly, Joe had done his homework; he had researched other companies and how they were using e-learning. Finally, Joe knew that he and his audience shared common goals, so Joe focused his presentation on how his proposed training solution could help meet those goals.

Joe organized his presentation by topics. He began with his *hook*: the potential first-year benefits (including cost-effectiveness) of this initiative to the overall organization. This was a great opener for gaining his audience's attention and demonstrating the relevance of the project to all parts of the company. The *line* of his presentation consisted of a definition of e-learning and how it could be applied to Shaw, some of the advantages it might provide, examples from his research on industry and business experience with e-learning (including his department's pilot training program), some challenges that might carry over into Shaw's environment and how Shaw was able to meet those challenges, and a reiteration of the potential value to the total organization. Joe's *sinker* was a description of exactly what he needed in order to institute an e-learning solution at Shaw.

Joe used a combination of oral presentation and PowerPoint slides as his delivery technique. "This was very well received," he explained, "not so much because I'm a very creative person but because we had just established a new corporate logo (you can see a B&W version in chapter 5) which I incorporated into the presentation. With the help of instructor Teresa Black, we color-coordinated the PowerPoint slides with the logo, which gave the presentation a holistic feel. They were very receptive and very enthusiastic as we left the room. With all measures I think it was a success."

Joe's right; his presentation had very positive results. "Even though I was asking for more money than folks were willing to commit on that particular day," Joe said, "they liked the idea and were very receptive to the expanded scope of what we could provide and the cost-effectiveness of it. We moved forward with an incremental approach; so, rather than take on the 'whole enchilada' with the first swing, we decided to cost-justify each area of training based upon need. We implemented the first phase on the twelfth of June (less than a month after his presentation!) and we're working on the business cases for the additional areas right now. Where we can create the good internal business cases, where we can cost-justify, I believe the company is ready to move forward. It's not always just the cost-effective issue but also can we provide training to people we haven't reached before through using newer technologies? We think we can."

When we asked Joe what he thought was the main success factor for his presentation, he responded that it was the level of detail he was able to provide by really knowing his audience. "We anticipated audience questions and addressed them before they were asked. There were a couple of times during the presentation when I was asked 'What about . . .?' and I replied 'Great segue into my next slide!' By knowing our audience and anticipating what are they going to ask, we were able to provide the right detail, the right information, at the right time." We also believe it was Joe's positive attitude and enthusiasm, coupled with and a well-planned executed presentation, that ensured his success.

Checking In at DD Inc.

Deborah Garcia, president and CEO of Digital Denim, Inc., leans back in her chair as she reads the latest edition of *Fashion Industry Trends* (*FIT*), the industry's trade magazine. Her face reflects concern as she reads that her company's biggest competitor, London Blues, is projecting substantial gains for the third quarter while DD Inc. is experiencing a decline in overall sales. "What are they doing differently?" Deborah wonders aloud, knowing that London Blues' previous quarter had actually seen a dip in sales. Deborah reads further and discovers something that had not previously been reported in any of the trade magazines that she regularly reads. London Blues had recently taken over a small, online mail-order business, Street Smarts, Inc., a casual clothing company located in Tyler, Maine. "Is there a connection between this acquisition and LB's sudden spurt? Are there other influencing factors?" she wonders. Deborah pulls her chair up to her computer and types an email memo to her directors.

Date: September 4
To: Directors, Digital Denim, Inc.
From: Deborah Garcia, President & CEO

Good Morning Directors,
I presume you've seen this week's issue of *FIT*. Looks like London Blues is moving into our electronic niche with their acquisition of SSI. They're predicting an increase in sales next quarter. With this new development, they obviously plan on giving us a run for our money in the electronic marketplace.

I'm sure they are still a long way off in topping our electronic fitting room and other amenities, but we should take this as a warning. I need a half-hour of your time on Friday for a brief presentation. If 11:30 A.M. works for you, we can follow up with a strategy meeting over lunch in the conference room.
Deb

Learning Check

1. What are four general purposes for presentations?

2. What is an inspiring presentation intended to accomplish?

3. What are two other terms for an influencing presentation?

4. What are some important situational variables to consider during the presentation planning stage?

5. What are two critical rules of thumb for planning a presentation?

6. Why are presentation designers also project managers?

7. What are some of the responsibilities of a presentation project manager?

Do & Discuss

Put yourself in Deborah Garcia's place:

- What do you think the general purpose of her presentation to her directors on Friday should be?
- Write a couple of specific objectives that might be appropriate considering the general purpose and the situation with London Blues.
- Are there any other design elements she should consider?
- Why do you suppose she plans to have a strategy meeting after her presentation?
- Do you think email was an effective initial presentation delivery technique? Why or why not?

Your (hypothetical) company's management team must design, develop, and implement a multimedia presentation to a group of potential venture capitalists to convince them to invest in your company:

- What is the primary purpose of your presentation?
- What secondary purpose(s) might also apply?
- Define your presentation goals and some specific objectives for your audience.

In chapter 3, we'll continue with presentation design as we explore what your audience brings to the table. As you read chapter 3, you may want to contemplate some of the human characteristics that affect your everyday communications with people at school, at work, and/or at home such as language and experience. Many of the considerations and adjustments we make naturally in our casual conversations are the same as those accommodations we must make in more formal presentations to an audience, as you'll see in chapter 3.

Notes

1. Clark Lambert, *The Business Presentations Workbook* (Englewood Cliffs, N.J.: Prentice-Hall, Inc., 1989).

Source of Quote

Karlins, Marvin and Herbert I. Abelson. *Persuasion.* New York: Springer Publishing Company, Inc., 1970, p. 122.

Chapter 3

A Is for Audience

PACT Model[©]

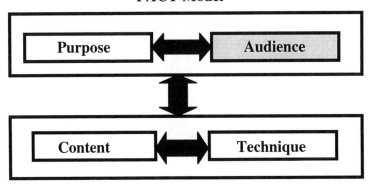

In the Do & Discuss section of the previous chapter, we asked you to ponder why Deborah Garcia may have chosen to have a strategy meeting after her presentation. We will speculate that the purpose of her presentation was a combination of informing her audience (key staff) of the updated facts on their competition *and* inspiring them to collectively and creatively tackle the situation at hand (i.e., in their long-range plans, London Blues may be trying to squeeze them out, and in their short range plans, LB will certainly outperform DD Inc. in the next quarter). Her strategy seems to involve more than just Deborah making a presentation alone. It also involves bringing her audience into her presentation in an interactive way. She is asking them to become part of the solution by having them contribute ideas, rather than autocratically presenting decisions to them that have already been made. How does she know her strategy will be effective? The answer is—*she knows her audience.* Audience analysis, the second component of the PACT Model for Designing Information Presentations, is what this chapter is all about. While purpose answers "*Why* do you need to design a presentation?" an audience analysis answers "*Who* will receive your presentation and what do we know about them?"

> *The people you may want most in your audience are often least likely to be there.*
>
> Marvin Karlins and Herbert I. Abelson, p. 122

Objectives

By the end of chapter 3, you should be able to:

- identify a number of important demographic variables related to a presentation audience,
- provide examples of how various audience characteristics can affect a presentation,
- describe several ways to deal with a variety of audience variables,
- describe how the presentation environment can have an impact on your presentation, and
- identify several constraints or barriers that might inhibit or prevent your audience from having the desired reaction to your presentation.

Keep in mind that throughout this book we use the term "audience" broadly. An audience is any person or persons who has some information gap or need; that is, some topic about which they are uncertain or unfamiliar. An audience can be a large group you face in a "live" oral presentation, or an audience could be a small number of individuals to whom you are presenting in a conference room setting. Your audience could be a group of trainees to whom you are delivering an instructional session over the Web, or your audience could be your CEO who is reading your annual report. Your audience might be comprised of the sales staff who will take the "canned" multimedia presentation you developed with them "on the road" or your clients who will view the marketing video you have created. As different as all of these purposes (as well as content and technique) are, there are a number of common audience characteristics that you will need to consider.

If you are making a presentation to people in your own organization, it will likely be relatively easy for you to find out some information about your audience. However, if you are presenting to an individual or a group outside your organization, you will need to do some digging.

Some suggest sending the contact person for the presentation a questionnaire about background information on the group and their organization (if there is one) and information about their needs, interests, attitudes, and abilities, as well as about the presentation environment, time constraints, etc. Sometimes you will need to use print and electronic resources to learn something about your audience. For example, if you are preparing a general brochure for teens living in New York City, you will need to do research on the needs and interests that are special to that group. In any case, you will want to learn as much as you can about your audience before developing your content and technique.

Knowing Your Audience

Knowing as much as you can about your audience will help you do a better job of designing your presentation. Factors such as demographics, personal baggage, prior knowledge and experience, cognitive style, personality style, needs, and biases, beliefs, and attitudes, as well as environmental factors such as climate, time of day, comfort, and group size may affect the success of your presentation.

Demographics

We will start with demographics because demographic variables are often the easiest to identify. Demographic information can help tailor a presentation to meet the needs of a particular audience. Some examples of demographic variables are age range, sex distribution, ethnic mix, group affiliation, group size, and education level.

Being aware of as many demographic variables as possible gives you an edge when presenting. For example, if you are preparing to deliver a presentation to a group of senior citizens, it might be useful to find out some of the key lifestyle concerns of that age group that may affect their perspective on the content you plan to present. A packet of print materials about an assisted living facility mailed to the home of some elderly relatives of one of the authors included information about such topics as transportation to and from doctors' appointments and religious services, medication monitoring, dietary options, and other information that addresses the particular needs of that demographic group. The materials were also printed in large type font, as senior citizens often experience difficulty in reading twelve-point font or smaller.

If any statistics are available on gender, ethnicity, or group affiliation, it will allow you to be sensitive to possible issues and questions that may arise related to your presentation topic. For example, if you are designing a brochure on health benefits for your organization and the majority of employees are female, you may want to highlight certain health issues that are of particular concern to women, such as mammograms and hormone therapy replacement.

The education level and prior knowledge of your audience is also very important. You do not want to talk down to your audience, and you certainly do not want to use jargon to impress your audience, assuming them to be more knowledgeable on your topic than, in fact, they are. In the first place, even educated audiences do not necessarily know the jargon of your particular area of expertise, and secondly, you jeopardize the success of your presentation by potentially seeming arrogant by assuming too little or boring by assuming too much about the knowledge level of your audience. This is discussed in more detail below.

While you may not be able to learn everything you need to know about your audience, finding out as much relevant information as possible will help ensure the quality of your presentation. In most circumstances, you will discover that there is quite a range of characteristics in your audience. This means that you will have to incorporate a range and variety of examples for your topic and anticipate questions from different perspectives.

Personal Baggage

Every audience brings with it a number of personal characteristics that should be considered when planning a presentation. This allows you, the designer, to create a presentation tailored to the needs of your specific audience that, in turn, optimizes your chances for making a positive impact. Some of these characteristics are:

- Prior knowledge and/or experience
- Cognitive style
- Personality style
- Needs
- Personal biases, beliefs, and attitudes

Prior Knowledge and/or Experience. Most audiences will already know anywhere from a little to a great deal about your topic. Others may have had no previous exposure to the topic (e.g., an emerging technology). Knowing your audience's level of prior knowledge about your topic is critical. Try to acquire this information before you begin to actually develop your content and technique. For example, if you are the new editor of your company's newsletter, you might want to go out and talk to a variety of employees to try to find out what people already know and what they might want and need to know. If you are giving an oral presentation and you cannot determine this information in advance, plan on asking your audience a few questions informally about their knowledge of the topic early in your presentation. This will allow you to make some adjustments on the spot, perhaps eliminating some of the technical terms or modifying definitions you had intended to use.

You might also want to provide an announcement or description of your presentation in such a way that potential audience members know whether the presentation would be appropriate for them. One time, one of the authors of this book attended a conference that listed and described a presentation she thought would be interesting. When she arrived she sat in the first row of the auditorium so that she wouldn't miss a word. However, she soon discovered that she did not have enough prior exposure to the particular research topic to benefit from the presentation. Too much jargon was used and no explanatory definitions were provided to help alleviate the situation. The presenters even used acronyms without explaining them! It was frustrating but it would have been embarrassing to leave since she made sure she had acquired a seat up front. If the description accompanying the listing in the conference guide had said something like "This presentation will be especially useful to those who have knowledge of X topic," then she probably wouldn't have attended the session because she didn't possess the prerequisite knowledge.

Another characteristic to consider is background experience. This might be job experience or simply life experience. If you are making an oral presentation at a staff meeting in your workplace or developing a written presentation to be delivered via your company intranet, it should not be difficult to make this assessment since you may already be aware of both the knowledge and experience that the employees possess.

Cognitive Style. Cognitive style is also an important characteristic to consider when planning a presentation. Cognitive style refers to the way in which different people approach, process, and respond to the same information. It can affect both the way individuals select the information they will attend to in your presentation and how they respond to new ideas.

People develop certain cognitive strategies to help manage their thinking processes. For example, one person might take copious notes while watching and listening to an important business video, with plans to review the notes later. Another person's strategy might be to forgo the notes in favor of listening carefully and possibly making mental connections with prior experience that would help with recall of the information at a later time.

There is a wide variety of individual differences in cognitive style among individuals. For example, some individuals prefer a broad or more holistic approach to the presentation of information. This means they might need an overview at the beginning of the presentation with details filled in as you go along. Others prefer to hear the details first leading up to the big picture or summary that brings it all together. Some individuals prefer to have the "big picture" on a topic, while others like to analyze the fine points. Some process visual (or auditory, verbal or written) information easier than the other types, while others prefer a combination of presentation types.

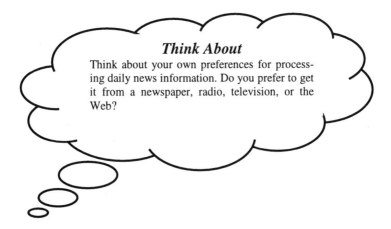

Think About
Think about your own preferences for processing daily news information. Do you prefer to get it from a newspaper, radio, television, or the Web?

Some individuals prefer to reflect on information as it is presented, taking time to mull things over. Others are more impulsive, reacting quickly to information input. If you've ever been in a class where participation is required, you may find it harder to do so if you have a more reflective cognitive style.

How might the cognitive styles of your audience affect the success of a multimedia presentation? If you are developing a multimedia presentation in which the user interacts with the system (e.g., an interactive Web site), it is possible to accommodate several cognitive styles by offering different tools for helping your audience get the most benefit from the presentation. For example, someone preferring the more holistic approach could be given the opportunity to select an overview of the entire presentation through a site map or menu before proceeding to the incremental sections. A more visual thinker could have access to graphics that further clarify salient points.

Personality Style. In addition to cognitive style, people differ in personality style as well. Personality style is the way a person approaches interpersonal interactions. One of the most popular and well-known tools for assessing personality used in business today is the Myers-Briggs Type Indicator® (MBTI).[1]

The MBTI was used as a way of validating and extending the work of Swiss psychologist Carl Jung who, in the first half of the twentieth century, identified specific patterns of behavior people exhibit when presented with information. Jung found that people either preferred to focus on taking in information (which he termed *perceiving*) or organizing and prioritizing information and making decisions (which he termed *judging*). Perceiving was described as either sensing or intuition; judging was described as either thinking or feeling. These preferences appeared to influence the type of information people attend to when they make decisions or solve problems. Jung also described two orientations (extraversion vs. introversion) with which people interact with their world and each other.[2]

If you decide you would like to know more about personality styles, you will find a wealth of resources on this topic in print and on the Internet. In your research, you will likely discover a variety of personality assessment tools that you might find fun and useful to take yourself. While identifying *specific* personality styles may be totally impossible with a large group, considering the *potential variety* of personality styles may be very useful when you are presenting to a familiar audience like your staff at work, your college fraternity, or your neighborhood organization.

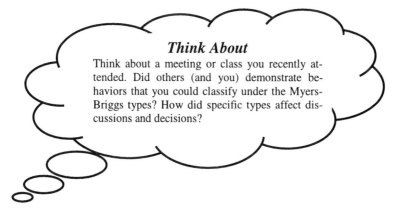

Think About

Think about a meeting or class you recently attended. Did others (and you) demonstrate behaviors that you could classify under the Myers-Briggs types? How did specific types affect discussions and decisions?

Just knowing that any audience (of more than one person) will have a variety of cognitive and personality styles to be considered will improve the quality of the design of your information presentation. While you cannot be expected to become an expert on cognitive and personality styles, having an awareness of the diversity of individuals across these dimensions helps you to become more sensitive in analyzing your audience whether your audience consists of ten employees in a conference room stand-up presentation, 150 readers of your company newsletter, or thousands of users of a complex interactive multimedia Web site.

Needs. The most general way of describing your audience's needs is by answering WIFT. WIFT is an easy-to-remember acronym for "What's in It For Them?" On the surface, the answer is often obvious. Common WIFTs include:

- They have an information gap that the presentation can fill.
- They want to be "recognized" by key individuals just for attending your presentation.
- They are paid for attending it.
- They can satisfy their curiosity about a topic. (This is a more intrinsically motivated WIFT while the others are guided more by extrinsic factors such as reward or recognition.)

In addition to the common WIFTs listed above, there are audience needs that operate on a much more subtle level. They are considered human motivations, and a theory that we find particularly useful when considering audience needs was developed by noted researcher David McClelland. In his research on *achievement motivation*, McClelland found that there are three primary needs that motivate people's behavior: 1) the need for achievement, 2) the need for affiliation, and 3) the need for power.[3] While each individual has all of these needs to some extent, generally one or two have the most influence.

For some, the *need for achievement* is very strong. These individuals prefer moderate (but do-able) challenges, work well independently, and continually set both short- and long-term personal goals. Let's say you were designing a hypertext information document and you knew that a large percentage of the users of the document would be high in need for achievement. One feature you could include that would help to satisfy this need would be optional "self-checks" throughout the document. (We have done that for readers of this book who are high in need for achievement by including a "Learning Check" and "Do & Discuss" at the end of each chapter.) This strategy works well for those who enjoy testing their own understanding of the information presented.

One who is high in *need for affiliation* prefers to work with others, enjoys the social aspects of the working environment, and seeks to please others. Those high in need for affiliation enjoy brainstorming activities and contributing to a group process, such as working in teams on a specific problem or project. We have attended to our reading audience's need for affiliation by providing group activities within the Do & Discuss section for several chapters of this book.

Flashback

Remember in the introduction to this chapter when we noted that Deborah Garcia knew her audience (the key staff members who would attend the Friday meeting)? From prior experience of working with her managers, she knew that most of them had high affiliation needs. While she could have presented her information in a memo or on the company's electronic bulletin board, she chose a face-to-face meeting format that included a participation component in order to involve her audience in an energetic brainstorming session. Each attendee had an opportunity to contribute to a group process that resulted in a plan of action to tackle the London Blues challenges that lay ahead. Her key players in the success of DD Inc. were probably much more satisfied than if Deborah had alternatively (1) come up with a plan of action herself and simply delivered it to her staff for implementation, or (2) sat down with each key player individually to assign them tasks for implementing her decisions (the latter would have been more successful with those high in need for achievement or power). Not only had the brainstorming session appealed to her audience's affiliation needs, but it probably generated more potentially successful strategies for dealing with the London Blues situation than she would have come up with on her own, since creative solutions to problems often emerge through group problem-solving techniques such as brainstorming.

The same brainstorming strategies could be applied to other information formats where an audience analysis indicates that appealing to users' need for affiliation was warranted. For example, a multimedia or Web-based presentation could be structured in a game-like way with simulations of group decision processes in a brainstorming mode. The user could provide his or her input to a brainstorming session and witness the result of the input on outcomes, that is, solutions to the problem at hand. This dynamic strategy is commonly used in group decision support systems and computer-based training.

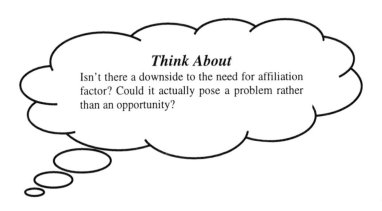

Think About

Isn't there a downside to the need for affiliation factor? Could it actually pose a problem rather than an opportunity?

You've probably been in the audience of a meeting or seminar where someone was constantly chatting with persons nearby. Unfortunately, high need for affiliation can occasionally be manifested in such negative behaviors. If exhibited consistently by the same person, the best thing you can do is recognize it when you see it and try to bring the person back to attending to what you are saying. How? Direct some attention in a polite way toward that person. You can accomplish this subtly, for instance, by asking the individual about his or her opinion on what you have said. The audience member will probably be unprepared to respond since he or she was talking at the time. Then, quickly take the focus off that person without embarrassing him or her. (You might *not* want to use this strategy on the chief executive officer or stockholders of your company!) You may have other ideas about how to deal with disruptive behaviors. Most presenters agree that it is important to remain "in charge" and handle people with dignity and respect.

You might think the *need for power* is a negative factor because the word "power" is often associated with self-serving, controlling behavior and manipulation. But a high need for power simply means a need to influence or have an impact on and guide others, hopefully in positive directions. In fact, many people who are high in need for power make excellent leaders. Teachers and members of the clergy are good examples; they are often high in need for power. You can easily see how they may use this power in positive ways.

Your audience analysis should be carried out during the presentation design phase. For print-based or multimedia presentations, there is no choice but to perform an audience analysis early in the design process. However, when delivering a live oral presentation, you should also be capable of analyzing your audience "on the fly," especially when certain individuals demand your attention in the midst of your presentation. That's when an understanding of human motives can be a powerful tool in your information presentation toolkit!

For example, the need for power can pose a potential problem when dealing with a live audience. Have you ever been part of a presentation or in the audience where one person is constantly challenging the speaker or asking for clarification in a way that intentionally makes the audience member seem to be more knowledgeable than the presenter? What should you do if you find yourself as the presenter in this kind of situation?

First, remain calm and keep in control of the situation. Now that you recognize this as possibly a high (although misguided) need for power behavior, you will know not to get trapped in a power struggle. One possible solution is to acknowledge the person's opinion while adding that there is often more than one opinion on the issue (then throw it back to the audience for comments). The point is not to allow that individual to take over, as weak presenters have discovered can easily happen. While we will talk more about personal presentation skills in chapter 8, this seems like a good place to add one more strategy related to being interrupted mid-stream by someone in your audience.

Certain presentations simply should not be interrupted (even by well-meaning folks) because of the resultant damage to both the flow of the presentation and to the audience's thought processes. In this situation, a good strategy is to ask at the beginning to have all questions held to the end of the presentation at which time you will invite a discussion. If, even after that, you are still being interrupted, politely address the person, telling him that you appreciate his thoughts, saying something like "Please hold that thought and we'll get back to it in just a little while." Then, wait until the end of your presentation (when you planned for a discussion anyway). By then, it is likely the impact of the interruption will have been diluted.

Personal Biases, Beliefs, and Attitudes. Quite often your audience brings with it certain prejudices, attitudes, or preconceived beliefs about you, your topic, or toward presentations in general. If you are able to learn what these may be, you can try to head them off. We often start the classes we teach by asking each student what expectations they have for the course. We immediately comment on each response, reinforcing realistic expectations and dispelling or correcting any misconceptions. If you were a manager presenting to a group of subordinates, your audience may feel that you are going to have unrealistic expectations of them or they may believe that managers don't understand their particular issues. To help alleviate these feelings, you might begin by clearly telling your audience what you will present and what is expected of them (making sure the expectations are at an appropriate level) and then describe some of the issues or problems that members of the audience face related to your topic. This would relieve anxiety over expectations and demonstrate empathy for your audience.

Environmental Factors

In chapter 2, we mentioned several environmental factors that can influence the way you plan your presentation. Knowing the size of your room and location, for example, are factors that would help you prepare the proper number of handouts for the number of people in your audience or the right sound system for the size of the room. Environmental variables can also affect your audience and how they respond to you. Let's look at a few of them.

Climate. When an audience receives a presentation in a hot, stuffy room with insufficient ventilation, it almost guarantees that people will become sleepy and have difficulty paying attention to the presentation. Presenting on a day when the room temperature is hovering at about fifty degrees, the climate will become so distracting that it will be nearly impossible for your audience to attend to your presentation. Controlling the physical climate of the presentation environment, whether it is a computer lab, an office, a meeting room, or an auditorium, will help eliminate the physiological barriers to effective information presentations.

Time of Day. Distributing your company newsletter during employees' lunch hour or presenting your annual report to the CEO just before he has to go into an important stockholders' meeting might result in a delay in receipt of your presentation or, even worse, your presentation being overlooked entirely. If the audience finds the time of day of your presentation inconvenient, they may be resentful toward it. Forget about getting a positive reaction if you make an oral presentation just before lunch and you're running long. Right after lunch, your audience is likely to be sleepy and inattentive. Early (but not too early) in the morning, when minds are fresh and people do not have to leave unfinished tasks, is often the ideal time for reception of a presentation (although we have found that this may not the best time to teach most undergraduate students).

Comfort. If your audience can only attend to your presentation by sitting at a computer terminal, at a table in a meeting room, or in folding seats in an auditorium, physical comfort becomes important. Is there adequate lighting if reading is required? Is the room set up with tables or just chairs? Are the chairs comfortable for sitting a long time (longer than an hour)? If possible, plan to add a couple of stretching breaks for lengthy presentations. If interaction among audience members is desirable, can people see each other or are they staring at the backs of heads? If you are delivering an oral presentation in which you desire participation and discussion, you might want to arrange the chairs so that people can see each other (it will be much more conducive to participation) in a circle or U-shaped configuration. Ergonomically designed chairs are essential for computer users.

Size of Audience. If you neglect to anticipate the exact (or at least approximate) number of people who will receive your presentation ahead of time, you may have disgruntled audience members, particularly if some receive handouts, newsletters, brochures, access to your Web site, etc. while others are left out. If the audience is a single person (e.g., your boss), you may wish to tailor the entire presentation to her. If your audience is the entire state of Michigan, you may need to keep your content as broad as possible in order to address the wide range of needs and interests likely among your audience members and you will have to select delivery techniques that satisfy mass communications requirements (e.g., television infomercial, newspaper article).

Consideration of various environmental factors can greatly affect the quality of your presentation. There are also a number of potential barriers that must be addressed for presentation success.

Hitting the Wall: Potential Barriers to Success

Each presentation has a number of potential barriers or constraints that can affect the way the audience receives it. This is an important, though often overlooked, audience variable. Barriers could include political factors (e.g., Does the audience perceive attending your presentation as advantageous or detrimental?), financial factors (e.g., Does lack of budget mean you cannot include information considered vital to your audience?), or even personal barriers (e.g., Are certain audience members offended by some of your content because of their personal belief system?). You will need to learn to recognize which barriers may be penetrable and which are not.

Let's Hear It!•))

The Community and Information Technology Institute (CITI) is a non-profit organization within the School of Information Studies at Syracuse University. CITI helps public sector agencies make advanced technology decisions. "We define public sector rather broadly," says Wayne Miner, CITI's Associate Director. "Public sector is not just government but it's also health care and educational institutions." CITI accomplishes its objectives through consulting, research, and technology transfer, working with students and with public and private sector partners on projects in these three areas.

What kind of presentations does Wayne do on behalf of CITI? "Most of our presentations are what I call either 'sales' or 'marketing' presentations," he responds. "When I say we're giving a *sales* presentation, we're typically talking to a potential corporate or government partner that would want to become involved with the projects we're working with and, hopefully, would provide us with funding to enable those projects to move forward. If we're giving what I call a *marketing* presentation, it's basically a presentation that addresses some of the activities that we're doing. Both our sales and marketing presentations talk about who we are and what we do and, if we're talking to a potential corporate partner, we try to address the benefits of the corporate partner's participation in these particular projects. If we're giving what I call a marketing presentation, we focus the presentation on some of the projects that we have in place and some of the successes that we've had with our projects. We let our audience know who we are and what we're doing and if we're giving our presentation to a government or corporate partner, the intent is to bring them onboard with the project and secure some funding." You might be thinking that Wayne's "sales" presentations are intended to *influence* while his "marketing" presentations are intended to both *inform* and *inspire*.

When preparing a presentation for CITI, Wayne realizes the importance of knowing his audience. "One of the things I do in preparing for a presentation is to try to understand who my audience is, what their interests are, and what common meeting points between our two entities might exist," he states. "Now if we're looking to develop a relationship, and that's what many of these presentations are about, you look for perceived mutual value or benefit in that relationship. That is what's going to make it a success, or what we hope will make it a success."

Wayne and his staff don't just depend on guesswork when preparing for an audience of potential partners. "Many times when we go into a presentation, we have a good understanding of whom we're going to be presenting to and what their interests are, so we do some homework in that area. For example, in a presentation we gave to Verizon, we went to the University's Development Office to find out who the company's representatives would be, what their job titles were, maybe get their bios, find out what their job responsibilities are, and why they are coming to visit Syracuse University." This research is time well spent: it helps them determine exactly what and how much content they need to include and what approach they might need to take with a particular audience.

But Wayne doesn't stop there. He goes right to the source to find out additional information. "I try to engage my audience in conversation first; I try to get them to talk about themselves. I try to get a better understanding of who they are and why they're here from a business perspective but I also try to get a better understanding of the person, maybe to understand what are hot buttons, if you will. Whether they are hot buttons associated with their business objectives, or they might even be at a personal level. Perhaps it's a very ego-driven person; I'll keep that in mind."

Wayne underscores the importance of good listening skills. "A key to any presentation is first to listen closely to the customers—what are their interests? I try to get as much information I can from them before I open my mouth to talk about us. When I create a presentation, it's kept somewhat generic. I always try to leave enough room to come back to the issues that they may have brought up when they talk about themselves, who they are, why they're here and, at a deeper level, who's the person, what motivates them? I try to engage them in any way I can. You're trying to make them a 'stakeholder' in the process. Once you've made them a stakeholder, you've taken that first step toward their buy-in to why they should get involved with you." By thinking of your audience as stakeholders, you can make sure that you specify how the presentation will meet their needs.

CITI presentations are given to a wide range of organizations including the state of New York and companies such as Verizon and Alcatel. While these presentations always have an individualized flavor, they share a common framework. "We start with a very high level overview: who we are, what we do, what's our mission, and how we achieve the mission goals and objectives that we've put forth in presenting our projects," Wayne explains. "Once we've given the over-view, we'll drill down to some specific projects and most importantly whenever we talk about who we are, what we do, we try to drive home the benefits."

Wayne uses a multi-prong approach for his presentation technique. While the main part of his presentation combines an oral presentation with a multimedia (PowerPoint) presentation, he also provides a packet of print information containing general information about CITI, some press releases or stories that have been written about successful projects they've undertaken, and a three-slide-per-page handout of the PowerPoint presentation so they can follow along and jot down notes or questions that they might have during the course of the presentation.

Wayne reports that while the results of the presentation to Alcatel were positive and CITI did receive funding, he characterizes the results of the presentation to Verizon as "so-so." He explains, "At this point in time they are not going to fund us, but they are still interested." Both presentations generally contained the same information, keeping in mind the particular audience, so how could they have turned out so differently? Unfortunately, despite the amount of time and effort you put into preparing and implementing a presentation, there are often factors at work that can affect your success that have nothing to do with the quality of your presentation. In this case, Verizon was undergoing some changes and, at about the same time as the CITI presentation, had temporarily suspended investing in any further University-related projects. Wayne adds, "The downturn in the economy has had a big effect on us."

While there may be circumstances beyond your control that can influence the impact of a presentation, it is always useful to spend some time after each presentation reflecting on what went well and what didn't. This will help you do even better the next time. Wayne puts it this way, "I always look at a presentation and ask: What could we have done better? How could we have done things differently? How could we have been more focused? Did we really keep our audience in mind?"

Meanwhile, Back at DD Inc.

Dan Bernstein is Marketing Director at DD Inc. Deborah has asked Dan to make a recommendation to DD Inc.'s top management team (five directors, including Dan) on ways to better market DD Inc.'s products and services. She asks Dan to present the form of a brief, written report.

As Dan thinks about his task, he considers the purpose of his presentation. While his report is intended to inform the other managers of his marketing strategy, Dan also sees this as an opportunity to inspire them about the company's vision and its potential impact on the world of e-commerce. He also sees his presentation as a way to influence all departments within the company to better market DD Inc.'s products and services through their contributions to the company's Web site.

Next, Dan considers his audience, consisting of Alexis Pollanis, Director of Human Resources, Jacqueline Cooper, Director of Information Technology (IT), Sean Fortuno, Chief Financial Officer (CFO), and Deborah Garcia, CEO. Although they all share a common goal of making DD Inc. a success, they have very different perspectives on how to get there and, Dan thinks, perhaps a number of other differences that may affect how they receive his presentation.

Learning Check

1. What are some of the important audience demographics to identify as you are planning your presentation?

2. Give three examples of audience characteristics that can affect a presentation.

3. Describe what it means to be high in need for achievement, need for affiliation, and need for power.

4. What are some environmental factors that could affect the success of your presentation?

5. What are some potential barriers to a successful presentation?

Do & Discuss

Now that you know something about analyzing an audience:

- What are some ways Dan could analyze his presentation audience?
- What audience characteristics might be most important for him to know as he begins the design phase of his presentation?
- What environmental factors might affect the success of a written report?
- What potential barriers might Dan face?

Your (hypothetical) company's management team must design, develop, and implement a face-to-face multimedia presentation to a group of potential venture capitalists to convince them to invest in your company. The presentation will be held in the company's boardroom. Write an audience analysis, including the following information:

- How would you gather information about your audience and what information would be important?
- What environmental factors should you consider?
- What are some of the barriers or constraints you might face?

Viewpoints: In groups of four, plan an influencing presentation on an issue related to information technology. Two members take the pro position and two take the con position. Present your issue to the class and see who is more convincing (we bet it will be the ones who are the most knowledgeable and enthusiastic about their viewpoint).

Coming Up...

We have now completed the design phase of the PACT Model for Designing Effective Information Presentations. Next, we'll move into the development stage by considering the content you will include in your presentation and the technique(s) for delivering that content.

The next three chapters are sequenced in the following way: organization, selection, and research. But you may wish to read them in a different order, depending on the way you approach the development of your presentation's content. For example, if you know very little about your topic, you may prefer to begin by conducting research on your topic, selecting the specific information you need and then organizing it for presentation. Or, you may know quite a bit of basic information about your topic so you choose to begin by developing an outline or other organizational scheme, selecting the information you'll use and conducting research in order to plug in additional facts, statistics, visuals, etc. Or, you may bounce around among the three processes as you develop your content. So, read the next three chapters in any order that works for you.

Notes

1. Isabel Briggs Myers and Mary McCaulley, *Manual: A Guide to the Development and Use of the Myers-Briggs Type Indicator* (Palo Alto, Calif.: Consulting Psychologist Press, 1985).

2. Cory Caplinger, *Myers-Briggs Introduction*, Aug. 3, 2000. http://www.geocities.com/ lifexplore/

3. David C. McClelland, *Human Motivation* (Cambridge: Cambridge University Press, 1998).

Source of Quote

Karlins, Marvin and Herbert I. Abelson. *Persuasion*. New York: Springer Publishing Company, Inc., 1970, p. 122.

Chapter 4

C Is for Content: Organization
PACT Model©

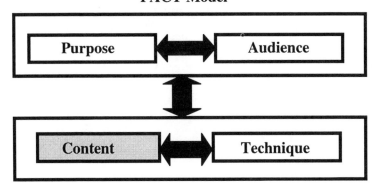

Now that you have defined your purpose and analyzed your audience, it is finally time to begin to develop your presentation. In this chapter, we describe a general, tried-'n-true overall organizational framework for the information you select for your presentation and several alternative approaches for organizing that information within that framework (we address content selection in chapter 5).

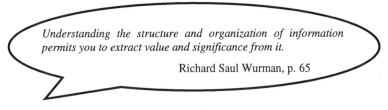

Understanding the structure and organization of information permits you to extract value and significance from it.

Richard Saul Wurman, p. 65

Objectives

By the end of chapter 4, you should be able to:

- identify the three essential elements of a presentation,
- provide examples of a good "hook" and a captivating "sinker,"
- describe the purpose of a "bridge" statement,
- explain what is meant by "capture the essence,"

- describe three main ways of organizing the "line" of a presentation, and
- identify three alternatives for providing order to the information in a presentation.

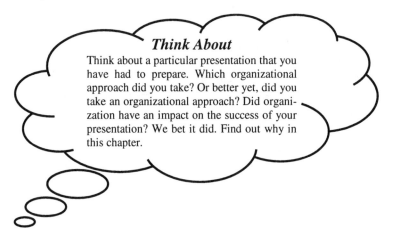

Think About
Think about a particular presentation that you have had to prepare. Which organizational approach did you take? Or better yet, did you take an organizational approach? Did organization have an impact on the success of your presentation? We bet it did. Find out why in this chapter.

The Essentials (Or, What You Learned in Elementary School Still Applies)

In elementary school, you probably learned that your reports, projects, stories, and so on all had to have a solid beginning, middle, and ending (perhaps you called them the introduction, body, and conclusion). Nothing much has changed; it all still applies. However, we use a fishing metaphor to describe these three main sections of a presentation structure.

The Hook (Capturing the Essence)

At the beginning of your presentation, you have several jobs to do and not a lot of time in which to do it. Why? Because an audience simply doesn't take much time to make up its mind about the quality of a presentation. The hook should also provide a *teaser* to the purpose and idea or message of your presentation. Don't beat around the bush. Be upfront, clear, and concise about your purpose, and be confident that your purpose is consistent with your audience's needs.

You have a few precious minutes at best. This is true no matter which format you choose to deliver your business presentation. The beginning of any presentation is of critical importance to its overall effectiveness. Your opening should accomplish two things: (1) grab the attention and interest of your audience and (2) capture the essence of your entire presentation. So, make sure your introduction *hooks* your audience by gaining its attention from the very beginning. A hook could be a provocative question, a meaningful quote, an attractive visual, or an interesting statistic that lets people know that what you are about to present is important.

Your hook should conclude with a transition or *bridge* statement. Like all bridges, it provides a connection from where you have been to where you are going. A bridge provides a smooth transition from the hook to the body of your presentation and must continue to motivate your audience to want to hear, read, watch, or interact more. It is a little like hooking them again and making them want more. You could simply tell your audience, "Next, we are going to look at several ways of improving service for our customers." But, we believe it's important to bridge to the body (we call it the "line") of your presentation in order to sustain the audience's attention and interest. Here's an example of what we mean. "In the next ten minutes . . . (or "In the next section of this report . . ." or "In the next part of this video . . .") I will provide you with six proven techniques that will improve customer service and satisfaction *and* result in putting more dollars in your personal pocket!"

Flashback

Remember WIFT? Can you see how the latter bridge will have a much stronger impact than the former? Your audience gets a sense of the direction your presentation will take and knows clearly what's in it for them. Now you have motivated them to keep listening (or reading or watching).

If you can do all of the above in just a couple of paragraphs or within the first few minutes of a presentation, you will have succeeded in the principle we want you to remember about a hook—to always capture the essence of your presentation right away. We use the word *essence* because it means getting to the heart of the matter, the gist, the kernel, the spirit, the sum and substance of what you have to say. Do not linger. Audiences often have limited time to devote to your presentation, so it takes careful planning for you to find a way to capture the essence of each presentation you make. But it's worth the effort and will pay great dividends. Capturing the essence is also a good principle to practice in your everyday communications. Learning to communicate your message with fewer words while making more powerful statements or arguments will increase your audience's eagerness to listen to what you have to say and make you a more effective communicator.

The Line (Reeling Them In)

A well-planned bridge or transition has comfortably brought you to the main part of your presentation. We call this part of the presentation the *line*. Think of a fisherman's line as the longest part of the presentation, used to *reel in* your audience to your message. The line contains the bulk of the content, arranged or sequenced in a smooth, logical, and interesting manner. It may include statistics, examples, testimonials, personal anecdotes, diagrams, pictures, humorous quotes, analogies, and other types of information that help to describe, explain, and enrich the basic information presented. And remember, these various types of information can also act as *motivators* to your audience.

Organization of your content allows your audience the ability to locate information needed quickly and easily. Imagine trying to find information on a specific topic by wading through volumes of an encyclopedia in which the information was organized randomly. It would be like finding a needle in a haystack!

Being aware of how others organize information saves frustration when you are trying to locate something quickly. There are several ways in which you can organize, or structure, your content. Wurman refers to them as "hatracks."[1] Your choice of organization will take into account your purpose, audience, and the subject matter of the content selected for your presentation.

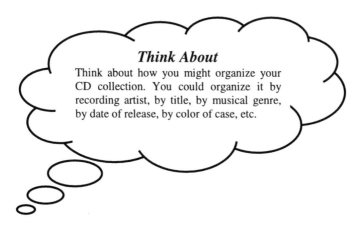

Think About
Think about how you might organize your CD collection. You could organize it by recording artist, by title, by musical genre, by date of release, by color of case, etc.

We present three general approaches to organizing the line of your presentation. These approaches are by Topic, Order, or Position. We help you to remember them with the acronym TOP and describe each of these approaches below.

Topic

How do you sort your laundry? Is it by color (i.e., darks, mediums, white)? Or do you organize by items such as all socks in one pile, all T-shirts in another, and so on? Most likely, you have your own personal organization system that works best for you, even if you do this rather mundane task without really thinking about it.

Information classified by topic is organized by similar importance. Think about the departments in a store, college majors, different sections of a project report such as budget, personnel, equipment, and so on. Even this book is organized by topic as we have broken the inforformation presented into several chapters. All of these examples represent organizing information by topics, sometimes referred to as "categories."[2]

There are several approaches to organizing a presentation according to topic.[3] One way is to present the *pros* and *cons* of an issue. Here, you would organize your information by providing statements for and against a certain course of action, followed by a conclusion that proposes the best solution. This approach is useful in influencing presentations, when you need to present the advantages and disadvantages of an issue in order to illuminate the rationale for your suggested course of action. The viewpoints activity suggested in the chapter 3 Do & Discuss is an example of using the pro-con approach to organizing by topic.

You could also present your information using a problem-solution approach, that is, demonstrating a problem situation and then presenting one or more possible solutions. The problem-solution approach is commonly used by advertisers in commercials and print campaigns as in the example below.

Got heartburn?
Just use Product X for instant relief!

Advertisers spend a great deal of money using and researching this approach and have found it to be very effective for influencing their target audience. In a business presentation, however, you will need to spend a bit more time making certain that you have clearly defined the problem before offering a solution. You may also want to present a number of alternative solutions.

Another approach for presenting by topic is cause-effect. This approach demonstrates that one action or event leads to another. For example, the American Cancer Society argues a causal connection between smoking and cancer. This approach demands support for your argument so make certain that you have researched your topic well. The result can be dramatic when done well, especially for presentations that seek to influence or inspire an audience (e.g., funding for a cause, signing a petition, acting on an environmental concern, following a leader).

Order

There are many times when we need to organize information for a presentation in a specific order. We have identified three ways of ordering information: Alphabetical, Continuum, and Time (we help you to remember it by the acronym ACT).

Alphabetical. You may have noticed that particularly large bodies of information are organized by alphabetical order. Some familiar examples include dictionaries, thesauri, encyclopedias, and book indexes. Alphabetical order allows you to easily scan content to find the exact information you need. It is a particularly useful way of organizing a large amount of information when you want to be careful not to convey special importance to one or more pieces of information. For example, a professor's class list will likely have students placed in alphabetical order. In programs at fundraising events, contributors are often listed in alphabetical order so it does not appear that one contributor is more important than another.

Continuum. This ordering method organizes information according to some pre-determined magnitude scale such as order of importance, smallest to largest, easiest to most difficult, least expensive to most expensive, etc. While a professor might list her students in alphabetical order, another method of ordering student information is by grade point average (GPA) along a continuum from highest to lowest. Diamonds are often categorized on a continuum using karat size or clarity as the order of magnitude. Movie credits often list actors in order of perceived importance (although it may have more to do with how much they are being paid to perform in the movie). Finally, if you are presenting a new concept or procedure, you could choose to present your content beginning with the simplest, most basic information and then proceeding to more difficult and complex information. These are all examples of organization by continnum.

Time. This approach organizes information by time (or chronological) sequence. It can be broad, such as past, present, future (or the reverse). Some topics actually demand using these broad time categories. For example, an informing presentation on the stages of pregnancy might start with the first trimester and progress from there. Other topics require more detailed temporal organization. For example, a checkbook is organized by specific date and check number. Sometimes, museum exhibits are organized in this way, such as an exhibit of an artist's work that shows how his style has changed over time. College transcripts are organized according to a time sequence (semester and year). Most history books are organized by time periods (from earliest to latest).

Position

Position can refer to geography or location. For example, most atlases are organized first by continent. The departments within a store are arranged topically (e.g., men's clothing, toys, housewares, furniture). However, if the store is in a mall, the mall's information presentation is typically organized by position; i.e., when you approach the information kiosk or open the mall's informational brochure, you can usually find a map organized by where each store is located. Sometimes, if it's very large, the mall map may be color-coded by location.

You may have noticed that there can be multiple ways of organizing your content. By using a combination of organizational approaches, you will provide greater flexibility for helping meet your audience's information needs. In our mall example, most information kiosks also allow you to look for similar types of stores (e.g., shoe stores) using an organization by topic or by store name using alphabetical organization. Your audience's information need (e.g., "I need to find a new pair of shoes" or "I need to find Minny's Shoe Boutique") will determine which approach is used. In our fundraising event program example, when there is a large number of contributors, the names may first be organized into groups or categories (topics) by level of contribution (e.g., over $1000, $500-1000, less than $500) and then alphabetically within each group. A book on American history might start with the discovery of America and end with the most current presidential election. Within each of those time periods, a number of historical events (topics) would then be discussed.

We like to use mnemonics and visuals as memory devices to help our audience (you) remember important information we are presenting to you. In this case, you might want to remember ways to organize in-

formation by thinking about how you want your presentation to be a
TOP ACT! Below, we also provide figure 4.1 to serve as a graphic
memory device.

You may find that you use combinations of organizational approaches for your presentation. For example, while you may use topics
as your main approach (e.g., issues to consider when building a house),
you may also use other approaches as ways of organizing the information under a certain topic (e.g., the order of legal papers that have to be
filed when building a house).

Regardless of the organizational approach(es) you choose, it will
be necessary for you to include information that supports your key
points. These may take the form of facts and figures, statistical summaries, charts or graphs, relevant events, video testimonials, empirical
research, or even personal experiences. Remember that the purpose of
factual support is not only to verify and validate your opinions or
statements, but also to add interest and make your presentation more
memorable.

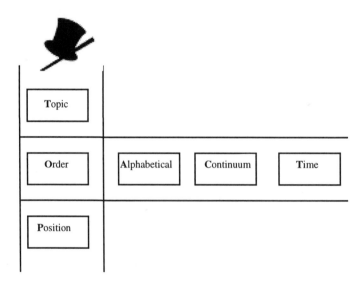

Figure 4.1. TOP ACT for information organization

Every piece of information included in the line of your presentation should help reinforce and clarify your purpose and the main ideas

presented in your hook. You were able to gain their attention at the beginning of your presentation and now you will have to sustain it. Even if your audience seems interested in your content, remember that it's still possible to bore your audience if you try hard enough! We can't emphasize enough how important it is to include some motivators to make sure your audience is interested and involved in your presentation from beginning to end (for a wealth of motivator ideas, see chapter 5).

If you are delivering an oral presentation to a live audience, you should be constantly aware of your audience's subtle cues about how your presentation is being received. These cues can provide a lot of helpful feedback. For example, check their faces to see if they seem to understand your logic; confused looks may signal that you need to stop, back up, and clarify what you have said. Try also to pick up on facial cues that may indicate how receptive they are to your message. Are many heads nodding and eyes closing? We give you more information about how both your own and your audience's body language and other nonverbal cues can affect the success of your oral presentation in chapter 8.

Remember the bridge to the line of your presentation that we mentioned in the section on the hook? You will also need to incorporate a bridge at the *end* of your line—the bridge to your *sinker* (i.e., close or conclusion). It should be brief but provide continuity from both the hook and line to the sinker.

The Sinker (The Power Ending)

Just as you had to spend some time developing a solid hook for your presentation, you will need to do the same in order to develop your closing *sinker*. A dramatic statement, quote, analogy, statistic, activity, or visual can all contribute to an effective power ending to your presentation. One of the authors recently attended a graduation address delivered by a well-known television talk show host. The speaker wanted to motivate her audience to "go out and change the world" through significant acts. She used a powerful quote as her sinker that summarized her inspiring presentation and effectively left her audience wanting more.

You may want to summarize the key points made in the line of your presentation and connect those points with statements about their

impact on either the individuals or the company, depending on your purpose. Or you might want to provide some type of exercise or activity that requires your audience to synthesize or summarize your presentation.

Remember to remain true to your audience analysis. Keep your audience motivated until the end. The use of high quality visual information to enhance your key information points can be a very effective sinker. You have this one last chance to pique their interest and achieve the broad purpose (and specific objectives) of your presentation—to inform, inspire, influence, or instruct. For example, your influencing presentation may have as its objective that the audience will "sign on the dotted line" and order the product or service you are pitching, like Joanna, our film studio marketing director's influencing presentation. Or your inspiring presentation may have as its objective to motivate your audience members to return to work with a renewed sense of fulfillment about the job they are doing, like our shoe department's inspiring presentation to her sales staff. Your sinker provides an opportunity for you to ask your audience to take an action, to feel a certain way, to make a decision, or to implement a new process. The outcome is dependent on both your purpose and your success in presenting yourself and your ideas. A captivating sinker can make the difference between a good presentation and a great one!

Let's Hear It! ◀))

Lucent Technologies is a "high-tech giant with a presence in 65 countries" and over 100,000 employees around the globe. It is one of the world's leading wireless communications networking equipment companies.[4]

Kerry Ryan is currently Manager of the Business Planning and Financial Management Team for Lucent's Mobile Internet Unit. When she was Portfolio Manager in the Service Provider Corporate Information Office (CIO), Kerry prepared and delivered an influencing presentation on a process they had developed for managing a portfolio of IT investments, as part of Lucent's executive leadership development program. The audience was comprised of approximately twenty members of the CIO, the information systems group at Lucent, including several vice presidents, senior managers, and directors. "In my previous role here, I managed a portfolio of IT applications the same way fund managers at a bank or financial institution would manage their own fund. As part of that, we needed to come up with some rationale and processes for how we would do this in the IT space. At that time it was a fairly new concept and there wasn't necessarily a right way or a wrong way to do it. So, for our presentation we looked at the various disciplines that were doing portfolio management, for example R&D and banking, and how we would apply that to information technology."

Kerry's presentation team consisted of four people. While all four contributed to the content of the presentation, only two team members (those with the strongest presentation skills) actually orally presented in order to prevent confusion for their audience. The oral presenters were Kerry and someone from Lucent's Corporate Finance Office (CFO), a finance person who could talk about dollar savings and provide statistical information. The presentation was twenty minutes long with an additional ten minute question-and-answer period.

Kerry's team organized the content of their presentation by topics, beginning with the need in order to justify its value and cost. They then described the process and the concepts and values within it. They concluded their presentation with information about how to actually implement the process and described what was needed to make it work.

There were several critical pieces of information included in the team's presentation: statistical information, gathered from various questionnaires administered within Lucent and to external benchmark companies, and a research piece. Their sources were professional and trade journals, popular news sources, and some academic sources.

"The third piece was what I'll call a 'birds of a feather' where we brought together the IT departments of some external companies and talked about some of these concepts. This contributed to the qualitative piece of our story. Then there was a more Lucent-specific or creative piece in terms of how we apply this to a particular group with all of these various quandaries that the organization faces every day," Kerry explained.

Kerry and her team didn't rely on oral information alone for their presentation. Kerry explained, "We shared a written report that included all the details that you couldn't really cover in a twenty-minute presentation. We also had a PowerPoint presentation and printed out the notes' section that included some of the details from the actual presentation. Usually when we worked on a PowerPoint presentation, it would have two or three bullet points on each slide but then when you speak to each of them there were different concepts associated with them. The notes' printouts were handed out to the audience members so that when they took them away if they wanted to reflect on the presentation they could go back and look at specific points."

While Kerry was an experienced presenter, she and her co-presenter didn't leave anything to chance. They conducted a formative evaluation by practicing their presentation in front of small groups and to their peers and modifying their presentation based on feedback from these sessions. "Unfortunately," Kerry relates, "once we got in front of this upper-level audience, my partner got a little nervous and repeated himself. He used index cards; I think that's fine especially when you're talking about specific sets of numbers and you need the details behind that. With Power Point you can't put up *all* of your results, like an Excel spreadsheet; nobody can read it anyway."

When asked why all their practicing didn't seem to relieve her partner's nervousness, Kerry replied, "My take on it is typically when a presentation is made to a group of people here at Lucent it tends to be more conversational. This was a formal presentation. In conversational presentations, you tend to get more feedback and people interject their own knowledge. In formal presentations, you don't get that. I know his style is very conversational and I think maybe that transition didn't work well. But during the question-and-answer period, he was great!"

What was the result of their presentation? "Usually we're asked to start using the model we proposed in a small setting and see how it works. We also needed to explore how we could partner effectively with groups outside of CIO in order to get some of our recommendations implemented. You can't just operate in isolation from the rest of the company. Part of the reason it was good to have the leadership there was that it helped to facilitate that partnership; in a hierarchical company sometimes it's difficult to call someone up and say 'Hi I need your help!' and give them some more action items to work on."

Finally, there was one unanticipated outcome that Kerry mentioned. "While we didn't necessarily use the process at our level, they adopted something similar at a higher level, focusing more on the financial pieces than some of the IT value pieces we talked about." The presentation was also developed to serve as a "road show" to take to different groups who are interested in the idea and talk to them about it. Once the concept was accepted by the higher-level community, it became more of an educational process to trickle it back into the organization.

We wondered what one factor Kerry thought contributed most to the success of their presentation. Her answer might surprise you. "I've worked on presentations where the only source of information you have is some existing literature and studies and things like that. But to have a quantitative piece in there really puts *umpff* behind what it is you're trying to get across; numbers are what people really pay attention to. And I think it's hard for a lot of people to ignore numbers. It allows people to reflect on whether or not it is a valid concept that you are proposing. That's important especially if you can break it down quantitatively not only in terms of what your competition is doing but also in terms of dollars. They're always going to ask 'Why should I do this?

What's the ultimate outcome going to be; am I going to save money? Or, am I going to make more money?' So that's why you need the numbers." Do you think Kerry's answer would have been the same if she had presented to a nonprofit social service agency or the faculty of a public school? Different content forms (e.g., visual, numerical information) may assume different levels of importance, depending on your audience. We address this very topic in chapter 5.

Show Me the Money at DD Inc.

Sean Fortuno, Chief Financial Officer (CFO) at DD Inc., is preparing to present his financial report to the annual meeting of stockholders of the company. He knows his purpose is to inform his target audience. He also knows that the audience will be comprised of a diverse group of investors who, while eager to hear how the new online venture has fared over the previous year, may have limited knowledge about various types of financial information. So Sean needs to organize his presentation in a way that provides a logical and understandable structure for his audience. Furthermore, knowing that financial information can be boring to some people, Sean wants to be sure that the structure he chooses engages his audience. He ponders the various ways for organizing his content.

Learning Check

1. What are the three essential elements of a presentation?

2. What are some examples of an effective hook?

3. What is meant by *capture the essence*?

4. Describe three main ways of organizing the line of a presentation.

5. What are the three alternatives for providing order to the information in a presentation?

6. What is a bridge statement and when should one be used?

Do & Discuss

Sean Fortuno could use some help organizing his financial report to the stockholders of DD Inc.:

- What way(s) might he organize his presentation?
- How can organization also be used to engage his audience?

Think about presentations for which you have been part of the audience. They can be any format—written reports, video, oral, etc. Then:

- Describe an example for each of the types of presentation organizations (topic, order, position) described in this chapter.
- Now describe an example of presentation organizations for each type of order (alphabetical, continuum, time).

As you begin to organize the information for your (hypothetical) company's management team's face-to-face multimedia presentation:

- What organizational approach(es) will work best for your information?
- Will you use a combination of approaches? If so, which ones?

You have identified your purpose, analyzed your audience, and have developed an organization for your content. Keeping organization in mind, it is now time to select the actual content you will include in your presentation. While this may seem simple enough (particularly if you already know a lot about your topic), there are many issues and many types of information to consider for selection. That is the subject of chapter 5.

Notes

1. Richard Saul Wurman, *Information Anxiety* (New York: Bantam Books, 1990).
2. Wurman, 59.
3. Jan D'Arcy, "Organizing Your Content," *Technically Speaking: Proven Ways to Make Your Next Presentation a Success* (New York: American Management Association, 1992), pp. 127-138.
4. *Lucent Technologies Web Site*, 2001. http://www.lucent.com.

Source of Quote

Wurman, Richard Saul. *Information Anxiety*. New York: Bantam Books, 1990.

Chapter 5

C Is for Content: Selection

PACT Model©

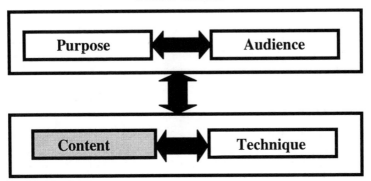

Once you have an organizational framework for your presentation, it's time to decide what content you will plug into that framework. In this chapter we describe the three basic types of information elements that comprise your content, discuss a number of considerations for adding value to these elements, and identify a variety of forms that your content might take.

> *The difference between the right word and the almost right word is the difference between lightning and the lightning bug.*
>
> Mark Twain

Objectives

By the end of chapter 5, you should be able to:

- identify the three types of information,

- define the amount and scope of the information selected for a presentation,
- describe several ways to add value to presentation information, and
- describe the alternative forms for presentation content and when each is most appropriate.

From Purpose Identification and Audience Analysis to Content Development

If you have done a thorough job of design, the next stage—organization and selection of your content—should go pretty smoothly. First, you must be true to the overall purpose of your presentation. For example, if your presentation is simply meant to be informative, do not waste too much time on presenting convincing arguments or injecting inspiring remarks on the benefits of the new information. Chances are your audience just wants the basics and will appreciate your expediency in delivering only the necessary core information.

Once you have created an organizational structure for your content, you will begin choosing the information you want to include in it. Here's another place where your audience analysis is important because the selection of your content may be determined, in part, by the results of that analysis. To the best of your knowledge, you have discerned what they are expecting of you and your presentation, their incoming attitudes toward your subject matter, their baseline knowledge level on your topic, what, if any, barriers or constraints you may encounter, and so on.

Choosing Your Information

While keeping in mind your purpose and audience, you must then make choices about your overall content, such as *what types* of information to include, *how much* information to include, *the scope* of that information, how to *add value* to the information you select, and in what *form(s)* your content will be. We discuss each of these in the following sections of this chapter.

Types of Information: Information Elements

After you have decided on (or have been assigned) the topic of your presentation, you will begin selecting or creating the types of information to include. We have identified three types of information, which we call *information elements*. First, there are the *core* information elements of a presentation. Core information elements are generally expository statements comprised of facts, concepts, principles, procedures, and/or opinions that present the basic information you wish your audience to have. Your presentation will likely contain combinations of core information types.

You may then add *clarifying* information elements that help further describe or provide a context for the core information. Clarifying information elements help to explain the core information elements and may provide opportunities for application and informational feedback. Some clarifying elements include examples, analogies, alternative representations, facts and statistics that support your ideas, definitions, details, demonstrations, personal anecdotes, case studies, summaries, visuals (for abstract or complex concepts), questioning, highlighting important information, and hands-on practice.

Finally, you may include *enriching* information elements that make a presentation more exciting and motivating for your audience. Enriching information elements add interest to both the core and clarifying information elements. Some examples of enriching elements are attention-focusing devices (e.g., change in voice tone, arrows, highlighting, color, graphics, graphs, charts, etc.), memory devices (e.g., mnemonics like TOP ACT and, later in this chapter, the 4 Cs of Quality—Correctness, Completeness, Currency, and Credibility), questions (actual or rhetorical), testimonials, and thought-provoking information such as incongruous statements or startling statistics.

Read the following brief information presentation about a breed of dog called the Skipperpoo (of course, we've made it up but let's proceed as if it were a real breed). The presentation's purpose is to inform. Its intended audience is prospective dog owners, breeders, and dog lovers in general. See if you can identify the core information elements, the clarifying elements, and the enriching information elements.

The Skipperpoo

The Skipperpoo is a small, long-tailed dog that looks something like a miniature Labrador retriever. The dog possesses a distinctive thick, shiny, black coat. It is intelligent, confident, and highly curious, as well as energetic and playful.

The Skipperpoo's expression is alert, questioning, and mischievous. Because of their intelligence and confidence, they make excellent watchdogs and are highly protective of their humans. Skipperpoos love to play and make wonderful family pets.

Skipperpoos originated in England in the eighteenth century. Because of their graceful, elegant way of moving, Skipperpoos were often the favorite of British royalty, who used them as coach dogs. Skipperpoos are Britain's most popular breed of hunting dog; their petite, wiry bodies allow them to chase small game into holes and tree trunks. The Earl of Buckham recently nominated Skipperpoos as England's national dog.

In this brief information presentation, the first paragraph provides the core information; i.e., you know the basics about what a Skipperpoo is and looks like once you have read it. The second paragraph and the picture clarify the core information; i.e., they further describe the Skipperpoo's appearance and personality. Finally, the last paragraph provides enriching information, i.e., information that, while not central to gaining basic knowledge about the topic, makes the content more interesting.

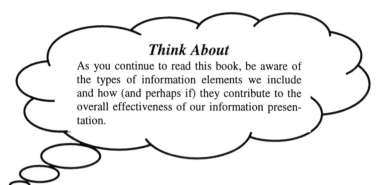

Think About

As you continue to read this book, be aware of the types of information elements we include and how (and perhaps if) they contribute to the overall effectiveness of our information presentation.

Amount and Scope

Another content selection decision concerns the *amount* of information to include in a presentation. For instance, you might want to have a large number of clarifying elements if the content is particularly abstract or difficult or if it is new to your audience; you might want a large number of enriching elements if the audience is particularly knowledgeable about the topic and you want to be sure to keep your audience interested and involved.

In addition to amount, you will want to decide on the scope (breadth and depth) of information to include. For instance, you may want to focus on a narrow scope of core information that you present in depth with a great deal of clarifying and enriching information, or you may want to focus on a greater amount of core information with only some clarifying and little or no enriching information. You could also present a broad overview of a topic and then focus the presentation on a single part of that topic; for example, you might present an overview (core information) on the broader issue of copyright and then focus on one specific case of copyright infringement on the Internet (clarifying information with perhaps some enriching information).

Adding Value

Every information presentation designer wants audience members to walk away from his or her presentation feeling satisfied that their information needs have been met and their time was well spent. That requires finding ways to stimulate your audience's interest while responding to the WIFT issue through relevant, meaningful information. You will also want to assure your audience that the content presented is easy to use and understandable. But how do you select information that addresses these issues?

We turn to the work of Robert Taylor in information science for some guidance. Taylor developed his Value-Added Model in 1986 to help describe ways to add value to an information system.[1] By defining a presentation as a type of information system, we use Taylor's model to identify ways to add value to that system.

Taylor designates three parts to the information process: *user, interface*, and *system*. The user is characterized as an active information seeker. In the context of information presentations, the users would be your audience.

Taylor defines the system as "a coherent series of value-added processes producing varying outputs."[2] In our context the information system would be the presentation itself. According to Taylor, the interface is the *negotiating space* between user and system. In a presentation context, if you were designing a Web site, for example, the Web would be the user interface, while in an oral presentation, you (the presenter) are the interface between user and system.

Taylor's Value-Added Model identifies a number of criteria that users value and ways both the interface and system can respond to those criteria. We believe these criteria are critical factors when designing information presentations. They include quality, noise reduction, adaptability, ease of use, and time- and cost-saving. Let's consider each of these in our presentation context.

Quality

Assuming the quality of any information presentation should be of primary importance to both the presentation designer and the presentation Audience, we define quality (based on Taylor's work) in terms of four criteria, which we call "the 4 Cs": *correctness, completeness, currency,* and *credibility*.

Correctness. Taylor says that if an information system is high in accuracy, the user will trust the system. The same may be said for an information presentation. Therefore, such activities as proofreading and editing contribute to a high mark on accuracy for your presentation. It is difficult for an audience to care about a presentation that is full of incorrect information.

Completeness. If critical core information is left out of a presentation, the audience will likely become confused and dissatisfied. A comprehensive presentation includes *all* of the information that is required to make that presentation a success for your audience. This may require the inclusion of both clarifying and enriching information. For example, for a historian writing a history book, coverage may need to be extensive with a great deal of clarifying information to explain certain historical events and enriching information to make the content more interesting. For a manager creating a report to his or her superior, selecting the amount and type of information to include will likely be more exclusive, focusing on presenting core information with some clarifying information where needed and little or no enriching information. References to source materials used in a presentation must also be correct and complete.

Currency. Currency refers to the up-to-date nature of the information you include in your presentation. A Web site that has not been recently updated, a written report that is seriously outdated, an oral presentation that includes information that is not current can jeopardize the credibility of a presentation and lead to a seriously dissatisfied audience.

Credibility. Credibility is largely based on: (1) the consistent use of reliable information throughout the presentation and verification of source material and (2) the validity of the information and information sources you use. The presentation designer's and/or presenter's credentials (e.g., experience, knowledge) can also contribute to credibility; that is, does your audience perceive you as a credible source of knowledge on the topic? Is there a way to contact the author or designer of a Web-based or written or video presentation to verify information presented?

Noise Reduction

Taylor defines noise reduction as a decrease in the excess of seemingly irrelevant information. A presentation containing meaningless or unimportant information will, at best, distract the audience from your message and, at worst, cause the audience to become bored or to misunderstand or misinterpret your message.

Linkage

Access to other relevant information is the goal of this factor. Features that facilitate access to specific information both within and external to the presentation (e.g., indexes, menus, overviews, pointers, summaries, hyperlinks) are important linkage considerations in the design of information presentations.

Selectivity

As an information presentation designer, you have to make choices concerning the "appropriateness and merit of certain information chunks or data"[3] to be presented to your audience. Selectivity should be based on the needs of your audience and requires a continuous process of filtering out unnecessary, outdated, and inaccurate information and incorporating additional useful information. An original presentation (e.g., a speech, report, Web site) may require a broader approach to selectivity than when updating, modifying, or expanding the original presentation.

Precision

"Precision refers specifically to those processes a system performs to ensure that a user has a high probability of retrieving information of value to a specific question."[4] This factor ensures that the information needed, and *only* the information needed, to communicate the intended message of your presentation is included. Extraneous or superfluous information that is not central to your content or does not contribute to the clarification or enrichment of your information should not be included in a presentation. This factor requires you to eliminate information that does not precisely meet the goals of your presentation.

Adaptability

Taylor describes adaptability in terms of the ability of the system to change and adapt according to the information needs of the user. Adaptability may be defined in terms of *flexibility* and *simplicity*.

Flexibility. Taylor defines flexibility as "the capability of the system to provide a variety of approaches for working dynamically with the data/information in a file."[5] Flexibility refers to the ability to change the amount, type, and/or format of information and the way to access the information in a presentation to meet the changing needs of your audience (or the needs of your changing audiences). Flexibility is possible in presentations that are fluid and organic such as oral presentations and Web sites. For example, in an oral presentation, if you added more clarifying information elements when you discovered your audience was having trouble understanding the core information, you would be demonstrating flexibility. For a Web site, allowing your audience the choice of receiving content in text or video form or providing opportunities for users to access additional examples or an expanded description of a concept would be examples of system flexibility. The ability to be flexible becomes decidedly more difficult with more linear, non-interactive types of presentations such as written reports and video presentations; flexibility may require waiting until you design the next version of that presentation.

Here's a real-life example of how important flexibility can be when the medium is inflexible. A Fortune 500 company paid a lot of money to an external marketing group to create a poster (approximately fourteen inches by three feet) that promoted its business support library to company employees. The poster was a beautiful piece, showing photographs of four world-class libraries, including their own. At the top of the poster was an inspiring quote and at the bottom was contact information about the company's library. A thousand copies were produced and distributed to all departments at their main headquarters and to other company locations throughout the country.

So what's the problem? After the posters were distributed, the company library moved from its location three times, rendering the poster obsolete even before it could be used! The critical contact information at the bottom of the poster was incorrect and the company could do nothing about it! (The idea of circulating stickers with the current, correct address was briefly considered but discarded because it was seen as too time-consuming and tacky.) The remaining posters were discarded. This was a very costly error.

Simplicity. Core information should be presented clearly and simply. This makes the information easier to understand and more efficiently used by your audience. Clarifying and enriching information elements should only be added to a presentation when they can enhance and facilitate the reception, understanding, and usefulness of the presentation.

Ease of Use

Ease of use refers to the relative difficulty the audience experiences when accessing and attending to a presentation. Some considerations for making your presentation easy to use for your audience are *formatting, ordering*, and *browsability*.

Formatting. A consistent, standardized format allows the audience to identify/find specific information of need or interest within your presentation. Highlighting, bolding, arrows, graphics, frames, chunk boxes (clearly separated sections of information), and tone or volume of voice are some formatting methods found to be useful in various forms of information presentations.

Ordering. Several ways of organizing and sequencing information were described in detail in chapter 4. Features like a table of contents, site map, menus, and agenda are methods for allowing your audience to understand the way the information has been organized within your information presentation.

Browsability. Features that facilitate browsability of an information presentation contribute to the orientation of your audience to the information contained in the presentation and their ability to explore that information. Some examples include headings and subheadings, consistent navigational buttons, screen design, indexes, help mechanisms, and handouts.

Time-Saving

Have you ever been in the audience where the speaker droned on long after critical information had been presented? Have you ever watched a video presentation where you found your mind wandering about halfway through? The amount of time required for an audience to experience a presentation must be considered when designing an information presentation. A Web site's response time for interactivity, the loading time for graphics, and the length of a speech or video are examples of time-related issues that, if not attended to, can result in losing the audience.

The consideration of factors that add value to the information within your presentation will contribute to the overall satisfaction of your presentation audience. There are also several forms your content can take.

> *Words, graphics, and tables are different mechanisms with but a single purpose—the presentation of information.*
>
> Edward Tufte, p. 181

Content Forms

When we think about the information we shall choose for our presentations, we often only think about the words (e.g., what *words* we use in our report or newsletter, what *words* we use on the screen in our multimedia presentation, what *words* are spoken in our oral, video, or audio presentation). Words generally make up your core presentation information. But what about clarifying and enriching information? It would be pretty boring if every presentation contained nothing but words. That's why few do. Just read a magazine article, look at a roadside billboard, go to a favorite Web site. We bet you'll find other content forms in addition to text or spoken words such as visual information, numerical information, audio information, and multimedia information. Information presentations frequently consist of some combination of two or more content forms. We describe each of these forms below.

Seeing Is Believing: Visual Information

Can you think of an example where you picked up a written presentation (a magazine, a brochure, a report, etc.) that contained absolutely no visuals? When is the last time you attended an oral presentation in which the presenter used *no* visuals in concert with his or her verbal message? The answer to these questions is, most likely, *never!* Most of us have come to automatically expect visuals to be incorporated into almost every type of information presentation we encounter. There are good reasons for that:

- Visual information facilitates understanding by illustrating or clarifying a point in a verbal presentation.
- Visual information can make a presentation more interesting and help maintain attention to your message.
- Visual information that includes moving images are more effective for conveying movement, growth, or time lapse than simple verbal description.
- As we found out in chapter 3, some people have a cognitive style that makes visual information easier to process than other types of information.

When preparing the visual aspects of a presentation, there are some related elements to consider. These are lettering (or font), color, and static vs. moving images.

Lettering

Often visuals also include words (e.g., titles, captions). When words become part of a visual, lettering clarity and readability become important. In written reports, for most audiences the ideal lettering size is

twelve point, although ten-point font may still be clearly readable depending on the choice of font (this book uses ten-point font). For projected lettering, the minimum size is eighteen point for a small audience (less than thirty people) sitting relatively close to the screen (e.g.,
in a classroom). In larger rooms (such as a large meeting room) with an
audience of thirty to fifty people, the minimum lettering size for legi-
bility is twenty-four point, while thirty-six point font is most appropriate for rooms holding up to 100 people. For audiences over 100 people
in places like large auditoriums, forty-eight point is preferable. Sans
serif fonts (i.e., typeface with simple lines and without those little
curly-Q's such as Arial or Geneva) rate highest in readability for all
types of presentations. Some more simple rules for projected text are:

- Use keywords.
- Include no more than six words to the line, six lines to the screen
  to avoid a cluttered look.
- Use caps and lower case, not all caps.

Color

Contrast and intensity of hue are important considerations when using
color. Beware of using exotic or unusual colors for projected visuals.
They might look great when you're designing them, but you (and your
audience) could be in for a big surprise when you project them on a
large screen! Some colors can look washed out and others may look
entirely different (e.g., purple may look red) when projected. Some
colors convey warmth (e.g., red, orange, yellow) while others convey a
coolness (e.g., blue, green, gray).

For most projected presentations, primary colors (blue, red, green)
are the safest. Colors should be harmonious and kept to a minimum.
Use bright colors in places where attention is needed. A good strategy
is to choose your background color first; then select colors for lettering
and graphics. For projected lettering, color is also a critical factor. The
ideal color combination for readability is yellow lettering on dark blue
background. Other recommended combinations are black lettering on a
white background or white lettering on a dark blue background. Avoid
font colors that blend into the background or are too bright or too light
and, again, don't use funky, offbeat colors for lettering unless you have
tested them by projecting them on a large screen.

—Presentation Tip—

Always practice a multimedia presentation in its projected form. This will allow you to see the effectiveness of your visual information, particularly the background colors and lettering, which can often look different in projected form.

Color can also be used as a means of emphasizing important information. For example, in projected visuals in which all words are yellow against a dark blue background, one word or phrase in red will stand out as especially important. Be aware that colors themselves convey messages. In fact, there is an entire body of research on the psychological symbolism of color (e.g., red communicates power, passion, or danger, blue conveys honesty and integrity). There are many books and Web sites devoted to describing how and what color communicates.

Static vs. Moving Images

At times when creating or selecting visuals for a presentation, it is most appropriate to select static images such as photographs or drawings rather than moving images like videos or animations. When using static images in written or multimedia presentations, be careful not to go overboard in the number of images used. Remember, a little goes a long way. Graphics like bullets, arrows, and boxes can be used to draw the audience's attention to specific information, while moving images like animations can be used to demonstrate movement or project change over time. Images should be large and crisp enough for people in the last row of the audience to be able to see clearly.

—Presentation Tip—

Each static image should be projected for at least five seconds so that your audience has enough time to process the information it contains.

Sometimes an entire message can be conveyed through a simple visual. Look at the following familiar visuals. We'd guess that it probably didn't take you more than a few seconds to associate the image with the message it conveys (you may need to allow more time for unfamiliar or more complex images).

At times, we need to have a single static image or symbol that consistently represents us or our message. This is often called a *logo*. When designing a logo remember that it, too, communicates a message, so it is important to keep it simple and memorable. For example, the logo (and slogan) below was developed for Shaw Industries, a major flooring company headquartered in Dalton, Georgia. Later, we'll see how this logo provided the basis for a highly successful influencing presentation by one of Shaw's managers.

While most agree that visual information can clarify or enrich presentation information, it can also be misused, often resulting in what Taylor would describe as "noise" (perhaps we should think of it as *subtracting* rather than adding value). For example, you shouldn't use visuals that:

- distract your audience from your message (subtracts from the *precision* of your presentation),
- are not relevant to your topic (subtracts from the *selectivity* of your presentation),
- are used only to fill time (subtracts from the *time-savings* efficiency of your presentation), and
- are of poor quality, making them difficult to see or understand (subtracts from *ease of use*).

Numbers Don't Lie: Numerical Information

Numerical information can add credibility, especially in influencing presentations in which you want to persuade your audience to a particular point of view or course of action. The use of statistics can provide evidence to substantiate and enrich a fact or opinion. For example, in a newspaper article the statement "Teenage pregnancy is still a major problem in the United States" was followed by this statistic: "Forty percent of American women become pregnant before the age of 20." While the first statement may be interpreted as simply an opinion, the statistical evidence provided enriching information that added strength and credibility to the story, as long as the source of the statistical information is stated and credible.

Generally, statistical information should be reported in aggregated, final form (e.g., averages, sums) rather than raw form. If your audience requests raw data (and it is available to you), you should put it in the form of tables in an appendix or handout or as a link, rather than in the main body of your presentation.

Often the most effective way to describe, explore, and summarize a set of numbers—even a very large set—is to look at pictures of those numbers.
Edward Tufte, Introduction

Tables, Graphs, and Charts

Using current spreadsheet technology, it is easy to create professional-looking visual representations of numerical data. Selecting which type of visual representation to use depends on the message you hope to convey.

Tables

Tables like the fictional one shown on the next page are useful for sharing raw data and for presenting several types of numerical information at one time. All information in columns and rows of tables should be clearly labeled. The table should also include an overall title to clarify what the table is showing and the source of the data shown. (Titles may appear above or below tables, graphs, or charts.)

As you look closely at our fictional table, you will notice that it shows the number of visits to the most popular Web sites (remember, our data are purely fictional). It also adds value to the data by indicating the percent of change over time for each Web site. Tables are good

The Top Ten Visited Commercial Web Sites for 2000-2001

Site	*Unique visitors in Feb. 2000	*Unique visitors in Feb. 2001	Percent Change
PACT.com	7,143,000	6,932,000	-3 percent
4Is.com	6,168,000	6,796,000	10.2 percent
TOPACT.com	3,880,000	3,029,000	-21.9 percent
DDInc.com	313,000	2,031,000	548.9 percent
TheHook.com	1,009,000	1,585,000	57.1 percent
Overlay.com	1,565,000	1,133,000	-27.6 percent
TheSinker.com	875,000	1,055,000	20.6 percent
SUCCESS.com	765,000	1,042,000	36.2 percent
Evaluate.com	**	946,000	N/A

*The actual number of people who visited the Web site or online property at least once in the given month. All unique visitors, at home and at work, are unduplicated.

**No reportable traffic

SOURCE: Make a PACT for Success

if you want someone to be able to look for a specific piece of information, such as the number of visitors to a particular site in a particular year. Data displayed in a table can be complicated, though, and there are other ways to show them.

Aggregated data are best represented in the combined text-visual-numerical form of a chart or graph. This adds value by making the numerical information easier to use and understand. We describe three commonly used types of graphs and charts: bar graphs, line graphs, and pie charts.

Bar Graphs

Bar graphs are used to emphasize relationships and show how items compare. Where needed, a bar graph uses a text label to define each axis. Numerical labels are used to orient the audience to the relative values of the bars. Text labels describe each bar. (Bar graphs can also be drawn with bars appearing vertically and numerical values along the horizontal axis.)

—Presentation Tip—

All graphs and charts should have a title that clearly identifies their overall topic.

The following bar graph compares the total percentage of DD Inc. purchases via the Web over a six-year period. The bars are presented vertically. You can also compare a large amount of data using a bar graph.

% of Web Purchases at DD Inc.

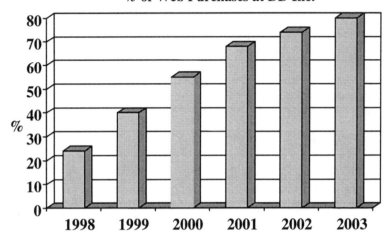

Our second bar graph displays how its local, regional, and national competitors rate DD Inc.'s Web presence in such a way that comparisons may be made quickly and easily. It also shows how you can graph bars horizontally.

Importance of Web Presence to DD Inc. Competitors by Location

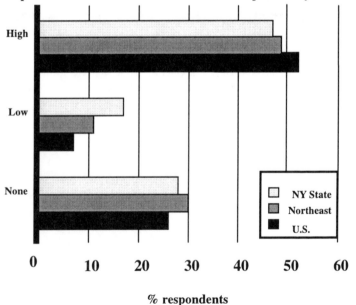

% respondents

Line Graphs

Line graphs are best used for indicating trends over time. Numbers are used to orient the audience to the values of each point on a line. Each axis should have a text label. It is often useful to provide a key for the audience to use as a reference for understanding the significance of each line.

It's clear in the line graph on the next page that over six years the total number of PACT Model users has grown in all three geographic areas and has increased the most in the United States and the least in Europe. (Of course, these are again fictional data.) The key appears in the left-hand corner of the graph.

Total Users of PACT Model in Thousands, 1997-2003

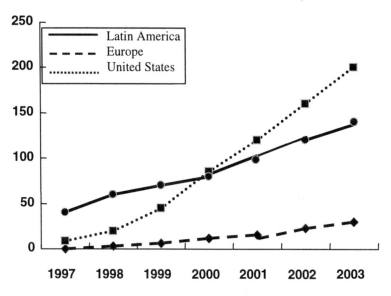

Pie Charts

Pie charts are used to display the relative contributions of many things to the whole. Colors, shading, and/or patterns are used to distinguish different slices of the pie, while text labels describe each slice. Numerical information (typically in the form of percentages) defines the worth of each slice, relative to 100 percent.

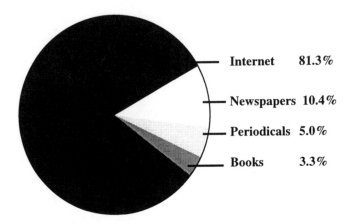

Internet   81.3%

Newspapers 10.4%

Periodicals 5.0%

Books   3.3%

Percentage of Sources Used for PACT Presentations

In our pie chart example, we can see the proportion of various sources for use in PACT presentations. Clearly, in our fictional pie chart, the Internet is the primary source used.

Flow Charts

Flow charts are used to show a sequence of steps in a process. The steps in the process are typically represented by rectangles containing the words describing the action and by diamonds representing questions or decision points. Sometimes, the beginning and end of the process are represented with a circle. Arrows are used to indicate the flow of the process. The following example uses this format to describe the process for completing the Learning Checks at the end of each chapter of this book.

Completing Learning Checks

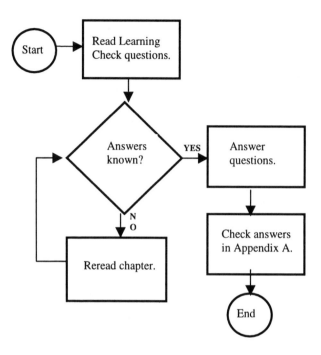

Here are some key points to remember when using graphs, charts, or tables in your presentation:

- Don't put too many slices (maximum 6) into a pie chart or too many bars or lines (maximum 6) into a bar or line graph. This makes them difficult to read and comprehend and gives a cluttered look to your presentation.
- Be sure to include a main title that provides adequate description of the graph, chart, or table.
- Include labels for all data represented.
- Written reports are perhaps the best format for the use of tables. They are somewhat harder to read and understand in a projected presentation and may require more time to process than you can provide.

Have You Heard? Auditory Information

As with other content forms, auditory information should contribute to the overall message of the presentation by clarifying or enriching the core information.

Auditory information is most effective in presentations where listening is essential to understanding the core information. For example, an oral or multimedia presentation on the subject of opera would be most effective if it included auditory information form, such as clips from an audiotape, CD, or video with sound. There are several types of auditory information that can be used in a presentation, such as recorded voice (e.g., Martin Luther King Jr.'s *I Have a Dream* speech), music (e.g., *The William Tell Overture*), and sound effects (e.g., jungle noises).

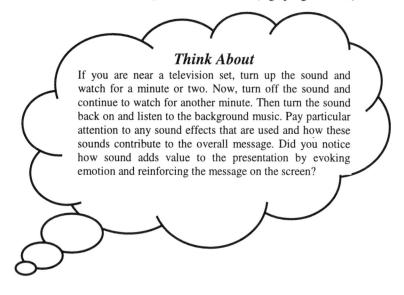

Think About

If you are near a television set, turn up the sound and watch for a minute or two. Now, turn off the sound and continue to watch for another minute. Then turn the sound back on and listen to the background music. Pay particular attention to any sound effects that are used and how these sounds contribute to the overall message. Did you notice how sound adds value to the presentation by evoking emotion and reinforcing the message on the screen?

Using Multiple Senses: Computer-Based Multimedia Information

Computer-based multimedia contains information in two or more formats—text, sound, and/or visual. Once you have established your presentation's purpose and intended audience, you will have to decide whether you are going to create something new or use existing multimedia software. Will it be a stand-alone presentation for a kiosk or will it be used in conjunction with an oral presentation in an auditorium or other venue? Will the information be presented in a linear fashion or will it be interactive and nonlinear? We discuss computer-based multimedia information presentations in depth in chapter 9.

Communication Without Words: Nonverbal Information

Did you know that in an oral presentation you often convey information even when you don't say a word? Some call this phenomenon "body language," referring to those messages you send with a look, a nod, a hand gesture, your posture. For example, standing with your arms folded in front of you while speaking to an audience may convey defiance, arrogance, or impatience. Your tone of voice can convey nervousness or confidence, sincerity or insincerity, enthusiasm or lack thereof. Your manner of dress can imply professionalism or sloppiness. Information about body language and other forms of nonverbal communication are addressed in chapter 8.

Information overload is not a function of the volume of information out there. It's a gap between the volume of information and the tools we have to assimilate the information into useful knowledge.

Paul Saffo, p. 30

Information Overload

Americans today are exposed to overwhelming amounts and kinds of information, frequently resulting in a phenomenon called *information overload*. While the amount of available information is doubling every two to three years, the rate at which humans can process that information has not increased. Furthermore, we have access to a myriad of information sources—magazines, newspapers, books, videos and DVDs, audiotapes and CDs, databases, email, faxes, Web sites, other people, and the list goes on.

As designers of information presentations, we must use the tools Saffo refers to in order to help us more effectively and efficiently locate, select, use, manage, and evaluate information. These are the skills needed to be *information literate*. Information literacy is an essential capability for citizens of the twenty-first century. Research skills are required for the successful creation and delivery of information presentations. More information about these important skills and how to use them to locate and gather content for a presentation are the subject of chapter 6.

Let's Hear It! ◁))

Not all presentations are delivered to a large audience; in fact, there are times when you may present information to an audience of only one individual. That's the rule, not the exception, for Dr. Jacqueline (Jackie) Belen, a resident physician in obstetrics and gynecology at a mid-size hospital in the Detroit, Michigan, area. On a daily basis, Jackie must give oral presentations to attending physicians on the condition of their patients. As Jackie explains, "The patients are those I have admitted or have taken care of, any patients that I've seen. Then it's a decision about whether to treat them and what plan to initiate. We give them background information, such as how many pregnancies, how many weeks pregnant, etc., and current information."

As we mentioned, each time Jackie gives her presentation it is to an audience of one attending physician. "We might be calling him or her in the middle of the night so we have to make sure that the information we present is the *important* information. If the attending happens to be in the hospital, then we tell him when he's there. A lot of times attending physicians come in during the night or are in surgery performing a hysterectomy so they put it on the hands-free speaker phone and I end up yelling things into the operating room while I'm down with another patient in labor and delivery."

So Jackie must present the new patient information to the attending over the speakerphone while he is in the middle of surgery. You're probably thinking, isn't that distracting? Jackie tells us that he stops what he's doing for a second and listens. "It is so brief that it does not interfere with the surgical procedure," she assures us.

How does Jackie know what information to present? "Every time I give the presentation, it follows a certain order," she says. "The presentation usually uses a common framework—we start by saying their basic statistics like age, what they came in complaining of, a little about their history such as number of pregnancies, and then my objective findings from the physical exam. I also might give my opinion of what I think the plan should be and the attending can either agree or disagree. I could say, 'I think she's in labor; I want to keep her here. What do you think?' Or 'I don't think she's in labor; she's pretty comfortable. I was going to let her go home and follow up in the office. Does that sound good to you?' I need the attending physician's permission to follow through on this so it's critical that I give him the important information in an organized and concise manner that gives him *all* of the information needed to make a decision." Of course, the outcome of each of Jackie's presentations is the decision by the attending physician, followed by some type of action (e.g., sending the patient home, keeping her in the hospital and starting medication assuming she is going into labor). Therefore, you might say that Jackie's presentation is both informing and influencing.

While this procedure seems fairly straightforward, things can sometimes go awry. "There have been times when I give the whole presentation and I've forgotten to tell the attending something and I've hung up the phone," Jackie painfully recounts. "Then I have to call him back again." We asked if there might be some way of preventing this by writing down all of the information before calling the attending. "Usually I write it down but sometimes, when it gets really busy, I don't necessarily have the time to write it all down. A lot of times I start writing up the patient's admit note that has all of the information that goes on their chart before I make the call and then I just follow that."

What does Jackie think is the most important factor that contributes to the success of her presentations? She answers, "Two things: You have to make sure you give them *all* of the information needed and the *exact* information needed. You don't want them coming into the hospital in the morning and asking 'Why didn't you tell me about this?' For example, there's a certain infection for which a patient can test positive, requiring an antibiotic during labor. I write that down on the admit note so I remember to tell him that when I call. That can affect your plan too because you don't want the patient to go into labor too quickly. You want the antibiotic to kick in first. You have to make sure you give the attending all the information so you don't have to call him back." Jackie adds, "Believe me, he's not going to be too happy about calling him back at two o'clock in the morning or while he's in surgery. If I'm giving the presentation face-to-face when the attending comes into the hospital, he may be looking at the chart while I'm giving the presentation. But residents must always give the oral presentation; we never just hand an attending the chart and walk away. Because I've gathered the information, it's my job to summarize the information for the attending rather than making him have to read through the whole chart."

We wondered how Jackie knows what the exact information needed is. Jackie tells us, "A lot of that comes with experience. Last year as an intern, I did these presentations all year." She smiles as she thinks back

on her early experiences. "At first you give them every piece of information and then you hear them snoring in the background. So we learn
quickly to keep it brief, succinct, and complete and limit ourselves to
exactly what they want to hear when they are awakened at two o'clock
in the morning."

While Jackie has probably never heard of Taylor's Value-Added
Model, she addresses several of its factors every time she gives a presentation. First and foremost, she addresses all of the 4 Cs (correctness,
completeness, currency, and credibility). She also must sift through a
great amount of patient information, focusing on noise reduction and
precision. To be a successful presenter, Jackie adds value to her presentations through simplicity and time-savings, including only essential
core information, and by organizing the information into a standard
format and order for ease of use by her audience, the attending physician.

Reporting Back to DD Inc.

Sean Fortuno, CFO (chief financial officer) at DD Inc., is preparing his annual financial report for Deborah Garcia, CEO, and
eventually another report to the company's stockholders. Sean's
presentation is intended to inform both of his audiences, but he
hopes to also inspire the stockholders with the excellent news that
the company has earned record profits for this year.

Sean thinks about the content for his presentation. The
amount and scope of these two seemingly similar presentations
are actually quite different. In addition to the core financial information elements, he wants to incorporate a variety of clarifying and enriching information elements, including a variety of
content forms. Sean has only a short time to prepare his presentation as the stockholders' meeting is in three weeks and his report
to Deborah is due one week earlier.

Learning Check

1. What are three major types of information elements for presentations?

2. What are some ways to add value to information presentations?

3. What are the 4 Cs of presentation quality?

4. Name at least two content forms.

5. What are some elements to consider when preparing the visual aspects of a presentation?

6. When is it appropriate to use a numerical table in a presentation?

7. Name at least two types of charts or graphs.

8. When does information overload occur?

Do & Discuss

Sean Fortuno has a major challenge—to prepare financial reports for the CEO (Deborah Garcia) and for DD Inc.'s stockholders. Perhaps you can help him:

- In what ways will the amount and scope of information for each presentation differ?

- Why do you think it is important for Sean to incorporate clarifying and enriching information elements into both of his reports?
- What value-added factors would be important for Sean to address in each of his presentations and why?
- What types of clarifying and enriching information elements do you think Sean should use in his report to the stockholders of DD Inc.?
- How is that different from the clarifying and enriching information elements he should use in his report to Deborah?
- What content forms would be most effective for Sean to use for each presentation?

Think of some familiar logos from companies, sports teams, universities, etc. Then:

- Discuss what type of message each logo conveys. Is color part of the message?
- Is the logo effective or confusing?
- Have there been changes in the logo over the years; if so, why?
- What might a logo for DD Inc. look like?

Coming Up...

Selecting information for your presentation may require you to do some research. Chapter 6 defines the research process in terms of eight general information skills. It further identifies a number of specific sub-skills within each of the eight general information skills.

Notes

1. Robert S. Taylor, *Value-Added Processes in Information Systems.* Norwood, N.J.: Ablex, 1986.
2. Taylor, p. 49.

3. Taylor, p. 61.
4. Taylor, p. 61.
5. Taylor, p. 66.

Sources of Quotes

Saffo, Paul. "Managing Information—Infoglut: New Tools Can Help Tame an Ocean of Data," *Information Week*, Oct. 30, 1995.

Taylor, Robert S. *Value-Added Processes in Information Systems.* Norwood, N.J.: Ablex, 1986.

Tufte, Edward R. *The Visual Display of Quantitative Information.* Cheshire, Conn.: Graphics Press, 1983.

Chapter 6

C Is for Content: Research

PACT Model©

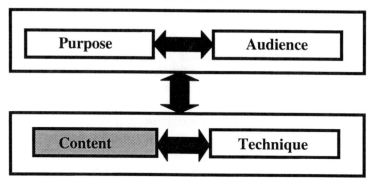

Consider all of the decisions we make on a daily basis—what to choose from a restaurant menu, the best way to get from home to your friend's house, which book to read, what elective courses to take, how to ask for a raise, whom to vote for in an election, what to wear, and so on. Each of these decisions requires information in order to make the best choice. Some call these decisions "information problems," that is, problems that require locating, understanding, organizing, and evaluating information in order to solve them.

Let's think of presentation design as a type of information problem. We must not only be concerned with how to organize our information and what kinds of information to select for presentation, we also must know where and how to obtain the information we need for inclusion. We call this deliberate search for information *research*.

> *Information literacy—the ability to find and use information—is the keystone of lifelong learning.*
>
> *Information Power*, p. 1

In this chapter, we describe the research process as part of a larger concept of *information literacy*. We identify each of the essential research skills and sub-skills required in order to complete a research task successfully and begin to develop the content of a presentation.

Objectives

By the end of chapter 6, you should be able to:

- define the concept of information literacy,
- identify three information problem-solving models,
- name the eight general research skills, and
- identify some specific research sub-skills.

Research: Information Skills
for the Twenty-First Century

Citizens of the twenty-first century must be information-literate; that is, they must possess the skills that allow them to find and collect a variety of information sources and be able to locate, use, organize, synthesize, communicate, and evaluate the information within those sources. Another name for this process is *research*.

Often when we think of research, we conjure up intimidating images of scientists compiling complicated data drawn from their lab experiments. Research can be as simple as asking a human expert a question or as complex as searching multiple databases for information on a specific subject. In essence, when we conduct research we are seeking a solution to an information problem.

There were several information problem-solving models developed in the late 1980s to early 1990s that provide a framework for developing research skills. For example, Mike Eisenberg and Bob Berkowitz developed the Big Six© Approach to Information Problem-Solving. This general approach to the information problem-solving process consists of six major steps, beginning with defining the parameters of the information task or problem, then identifying the alternative potential sources of information to help solve the problem, locating and using those sources, organizing and presenting the information, and ending with evaluating both the results of the process and the process itself.[1]

Another approach to research, the Research Process Model, was developed by Barbara Stripling and Judy Pitts. This model follows a more linear approach to research, using a ten-step process beginning with the selection of a broad research topic and getting an overview of that topic, narrowing the topic, formulating research questions and planning the research to be done, locating the relevant sources, analyzing both the sources and the information within them and extracting relevant information, and creating and presenting a final research product. What differentiates their model from the others is the interspersion of eight "reflection points" that allow the researcher to step back several times from the process momentarily and evaluate and revise what he or she has done or repeat completed steps where needed.[2] We think reflection is an important activity during any creative process. (The "Think About" feature included at appropriate points throughout this book was designed to provide you with opportunities for reflection on the content presented.)

Carol Kuhlthau's Model of the Search Process describes a six-stage research process. Kuhlthau's model begins with initiation of the research task, tentatively selecting a topic and doing some initial exploration, becoming more focused on the topic and research plan, collecting information and ending the search process, presenting the research results, and assessing the research outcomes.[3]

What differentiates Kuhlthau's model from others is that it is based on several years of research in which she documented the process students use as they conduct their research activities. Kuhlthau discovered that, rather than the research process being a neat, sequential set of skills, it is actually a learning process that is often quite messy and much more iterative (rather than linear) in nature. For example, Kuhlthau found that students often explore and collect information before they have formulated or narrowed a topic. She discovered that even when they formulate a topic and begin to explore information about the topic, they often must refine their topic, explore more information, etc.[4]

Kuhlthau's research also revealed that during the research process, students often experience anxiety, apprehension, and uncertainty because of (1) an inability to narrow their topic and (2) information overload. For example, while exploring a variety of resources for information on a specified topic, the student may find that the topic must be expanded, modified, or narrowed, or may find he or she has to abandon that topic altogether and select a different one.

Essentially, all of these information problem-solving models share a common set of information skills which we have synthesized into the following eight major categories across three general time periods— Beginning, During, and Ending the research process. Each information skill is further defined by a set of more specific sub-skills.[5] Using these information skills is often required in order to collect information that may be incorporated into your presentation (and help prevent information overload for you!).

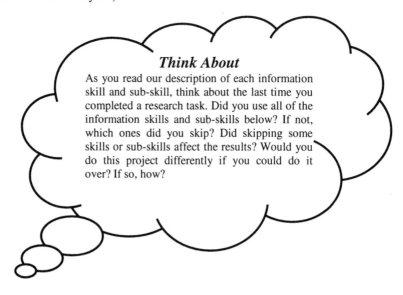

Think About

As you read our description of each information skill and sub-skill, think about the last time you completed a research task. Did you use all of the information skills and sub-skills below? If not, which ones did you skip? Did skipping some skills or sub-skills affect the results? Would you do this project differently if you could do it over? If so, how?

Beginning the Research Process

At the beginning of the research process, you will need to use Definition, Selection, and Planning skills.

Definition

Definition requires you to specify your information need or task and articulate your research goal(s). This is an essential first step; otherwise you could be searching for and gathering huge amounts of information that you will never use and spending more time doing it than is necessary. This information skill requires you to:

- *identify the specific requirements of the research task or assignment.* This may be provided in a memo, an assignment sheet, a syllabus, or a direct request from your boss or a colleague. If the parameters of the task are still unclear, you may have to seek further clarification.

- *determine the amount and type of information needed to complete the task or assignment.* Again, this may be specified by someone else (e.g., a five-page report) or may need additional clarification.
- *consider potential topics.* You must know enough about the general subject area to be able to brainstorm two or more potential research topics or you may be given a choice of topics. Otherwise, you will need to conduct some preliminary research on several relevant topics before choosing the one you will pursue.

Selection

Selection requires you to target a research topic or question to be explored. This information skill demands that you:

- *narrow or broaden the topic or question to be explored.* Once you begin to search for information on your topic, you may feel overwhelmed by the amount of information available. However, in other cases, you may find your topic is already too narrow and you will need to broaden it. Unless you already know a lot about the topic, typically you will need to do some preliminary searching for information on your topic in order to be able to narrow it.
- *specify subtopics or related keywords.* As you conduct your preliminary search for information, you may discover a number of more specific related subtopics or keywords to help you refine your topic selection.

Planning

Planning requires you to identify an information search strategy, as well as a range of potentially relevant types of information sources to explore. This information skill requires that you:

- *formulate a search strategy.* This is a plan for finding the information needed.
- *identify potential information sources.* Typically, a research topic may be found in many different information resources such as books, magazines, videos or DVDs, multimedia software, audiotapes or CDs, brochures, databases, human experts, etc.
- *create a general framework for organizing information found.* It is often helpful to create an outline or other organizing tool into which you can "plug in" any relevant information found during the research process. If you have already created an organizational scheme for your entire presentation (see chapter 4), you may find it

more efficient to refer to that scheme for plugging in your research findings. This could also serve as a means of checking to see if your organizational framework works for your topic.

- *identify potential formats for presentation of results.* While planning your search strategy, you may have already envisioned how the finished product will look and in what format it will be (i.e., your technique). Sometimes, the format is specified as part of the task parameters; other times, you must choose your format for presenting research results. For example, you may find that your topic requires a great number of charts and tables for which a written report is the best technique for presentation. Or, you may find that there is so much content in so many forms that you need to create a Web site with hyperlinks to additional information.

During the Research Process

During the research process you will utilize your Exploration, Collection, and Organization skills.

Exploration

Exploration requires you to explore, find, and use a range of information resources and to finalize the formulation of your research topic or question. This information skill demands that you:

- *access information resources.* These resources may be easy or difficult to access. For example, if the information resource is not readily available (e.g., an obscure journal, a book that is out of print), you may have to find other ways to access the materials needed (e.g., search the public library, use interlibrary loan, purchase the materials directly from the publisher, search the Web).
- *explore a range of information resources.* While certain types of resources may have large amounts of information, finding different perspectives or different types of information may require exploring a variety of information resources. For example, if you wish to create a multimedia presentation on the first Woodstock concert, you may need to explore newspaper articles from the time of the concert, books written after the concert, videotapes of the concert, interview people who attended, etc.
- *rethink the research topic.* Once you have begun to explore information on your topic, and especially if that topic is very broad (making the amount of information available unmanageable) or very narrow (resulting in very little available information), you

may need to reconsider the topic. You might decide to broaden or narrow the topic, you may want to group two or more related topics, or you may choose to change topics altogether.

- *finalize formulation of research topic.* It is at this point that you must make a final decision about what topic you will pursue.

Collection

Collection involves gathering and making note of relevant information from various sources. This information skill requires you to:

- *select the most appropriate information resources.* Once you have finalized your research topic and explored a number and variety of resources containing information on that topic, it is time to select those resources that can provide the most "bang for the buck." In other words, you must choose which resources have the best information for the research topic and the purpose of the research.
- *locate all relevant information within selected resources.* It is at this point that you must read, view, listen to, etc. the relevant information within the selected resources.
- *extract important information from selected resources.* As you are reading, viewing, listening, etc., you will likely use one or more note-taking methods to record and keep track of the important, relevant information you are finding. For example, you may take written notes on paper or note cards, type notes into a computer, or record notes into a tape recorder.
- *evaluate the correctness, credibility, currency, and completeness* (remember our 4 C's?) *of the information.* Either as you are extracting the information or once the information is extracted and you begin inserting it into your presentation, you must assess the quality of the information you have found, filtering out superfluous, irrelevant, outdated, or inaccurate information.
- *store gathered information for potential future use.* Now that you have identified the most relevant and highest quality information found, you must store that information. Note cards, file folders, and databases are three possible storage media for the information collected. You may also find that, while you don't use all of the information in your current presentation, you could use it at some future point and will have it readily available to you.

Organization

Organization requires you to summarize, sequence, and synthesize gathered information. This information skill necessitates that you:

- *analyze the relevance of information collected.* Again, as you go through this process, you are refining your topic so that it becomes easier and easier to recognize the information you might need and that which you can ignore.
- *filter out irrelevant information.* At this point, you must eliminate any information that does not add value to the presentation of your topic.
- *summarize and synthesize gathered information.* Now you must determine ways to complete the integration of the information from your notes into your general organizational scheme.
- *sequence selected information.* You must organize summarized notes into a coherent, logical sequence.
- *organize information for presentation.* It is at this point that you must determine a final organizational scheme for the gathered information.

Think About

Think about the large news media (newspapers, television, magazines). How are they able to obtain information on a topic for which they have very little time to prepare? What would happen if they had to research each topic every time a story erupted?

Ending the Research Process

You will use presentation and evaluation skills at the end of the research process.

Presentation

Presentation involves communicating the results of your research in the form of a presentation or report. This information skill demands that you:

- *select the most appropriate format for communicating results.* The presentation technique may have been specified by someone else or you may be given a choice of methods for communicating research results. That decision must consider whether a particular medium is more appropriate than others for presenting your topic and your research results. You may recall that identifying potential formats for presentations is also part of planning. (See chapters 7, 8, and 9 for more information about various techniques for presentation.)
- *assemble organized information for presentation.* You must take the information you have organized and create some form of presentation. Remember to reference your sources when you use an idea that is not your own and provide proper citations for direct quotes. Use an established notation style (e.g., Chicago, American Psychological Association) for citing references consistently throughout your presentation. References are a must, even for computer-based presentations.
- *present results.* You present your research results, adhering to any specifications defined for the task.

Evaluation

Evaluation requires you to assess both the results of the research process (i.e., your product) and the research process itself while determining ways to improve that process for future research activities. Therefore, this information skill requires that you:

- *evaluate the end product* (e.g., report, oral presentation, Web site). You may wish to create your own set of evaluation criteria or use a pre-existing set of evaluation criteria to determine the quality of your resulting research product. (See chapter 10 for more information on evaluation.)

- *assess the efficiency and effectiveness of the research process used.* At this point it is time to reflect on the process you used, identifying ways to improve for future research tasks.

- *determine the future usefulness or applicability of the research process and results.* You now understand how the research process can be used to solve future information problems or answer future research questions and have a file or database of information on your topic for future use.

These research stages and information skills and sub-skills are summarized in the figure on the following page. How critically and thoroughly you research your topic can have an enormous impact on the quality and effectiveness of your information presentation as well as your credibility with your audience.

Here's our job aid for remembering the skills and sub-skills required during the research process. You might find it useful the next time you need to conduct research for a presentation.

Research Skills and Sub-Skills

Beginning

Definition
- Identify the specific requirements of the research task or assignment.
- Determine the amount and type of information needed to complete the task or assignment.
- Consider potential topics.

Selection
- Narrow or broaden the topic or question to be explored.
- Specify subtopics or related keywords.

Planning
- Formulate a search strategy.
- Identify potential information sources.
- Create a general framework for organizing information found.
- Identify potential formats for presentation of results.

During

Exploration
- Access information resources.
- Explore a range of information resources.
- Rethink the research topic.
- Finalize formulation of research topic.

Collection
- Select the most appropriate information resources.
- Locate all relevant information within selected resources.
- Extract important information from selected resources.
- Evaluate correctness, credibility, currency, and completeness.
- Store gathered information for potential future use.

Organization
- Analyze the quality of information gathered.
- Filter out irrelevant information.
- Summarize and synthesize gathered information.
- Sequence selected information.
- Organize information for presentation.

Ending

Presentation
- Select the most appropriate format for communicating results.
- Assemble organized information for presentation.
- Present results.

Evaluation
- Evaluate the end product.
- Assess the efficiency and effectiveness of the research process used.
- Determine the future usefulness or applicability of the research process and results.

Let's Hear It!))

Alice Colasanti is a Contract Specialist at the Air Force Research Lab (AFRL) at the Rome (NY) Information Directorate, Air Force Research and Development Laboratory. The facility houses mostly innovative state-of-the-art research and development contract work for such clients as the Army, the Navy, and the intelligence community. The Rome AFRL (also known as Rome Labs) is one of four super-laboratories in the United States. The focus of Rome Labs is information technology while the other laboratories focus on such areas as biological warfare and medical projects.

Recently, Alice had the task of posting an RFP (Request for Proposal) to announce a particular program her organization was funding. Before doing this, Alice gathered together representatives from the various departments at Rome Labs to form a strategy panel whose mission was to reach consensus on the parameters and requirements of the RFP. Together, they would need to formulate a strategy as to what type of contract they envisioned, what the terms and conditions should be, and what they expected to see from the successful offerer. As Alice succinctly puts it, "Before we send the announcement out to the public, we want to make sure we are all in agreement as to what we are requesting. We need a strategy when it comes to the structure of the contract, both an efficient and legal way to get the best value for the taxpayer dollar."

Alice's audience consisted of co-workers, staff, and representatives from the legal, technical, budget, and contracting departments, a total of eighteen people. The presentation was held in a conference room and the audience was seated at one long, wooden conference table, which provided a more informal environment for Alice's presentation. While she delivered the presentation by herself, a technical team was there for support and to answer any questions she couldn't address. The room was equipped with computer-based projection equipment and Internet access.

Alice's two-hour presentation was organized by topics, and there were many of them. She led the panel through a thorough and complete set of issues that need to be addressed before and after posting the RFP. She began her presentation by giving the background of the technical effort from the time of inception, followed by information about the objectives of the effort, why they were going out with the announcement or solicitation, i.e., what need the government was trying to fill and how they envisioned that somebody can come back to fill that need. She then described the range of risks involved—technical risks cost risks, and scheduling risks—followed by the sources of funding, milestones, and business considerations (for example, some RFPs are classified as "top secret" and limited to small businesses). Alice then went on to talk about the market research, criteria for project management, engineering issues, past performance history, and policy issues such as cost-sharing. Alice developed her own method for making sure that all of these topics were covered. She used notes written on a colored, lined tablet, housed inside a leather folder. She says with a smile, "I use these notepads because I have a large handwriting and my eyesight isn't what it used to be." This technique allows Alice to have all the information in front of her, packaged in a way that appears professional.

With so much content to deliver, how did Alice maintain the attention of her audience? In addition to her oral presentation, Alice used several other presentation techniques and motivational strategies. We'll let her tell it in her own words. "I did an oral/PowerPoint presentation. I find PowerPoint, in addition to just talking, gets everyone to relax. I also provide the audience with one streamlined handout, a checklist of each of the issues we'll go over. They can write notes on it and questions for later if they don't want to interrupt. I also linked to a Web site so I could show them examples of some relevant, unclassified technical projects that had been done."

Alice also passes around a dish of candy at these sessions, chocolate-covered caramels to be exact. While this served to further relax her audience, Alice had an ulterior motive for selecting these particular candies. "I like caramels because once they pop them into their mouths, the candy keeps them from asking too many questions during my presentation," Alice admits with a laugh.

Actually, Alice encourages participation and reinforces her audience's value in the process. She also tries to use humor, wherever possible. She explains, "While this is very serious, I try to get the point across without making anyone feel uncomfortable because I need their input, a lot. I find if you try to act too superior like you know everything, and you can never know *everything*, then you have people who are waiting to show you that you're wrong. So at the beginning I try to say that 'This is what we're all here for,' we are just in the beginning stages of this process and I'm comfortable enough that I'm willing to change."

Alice categorizes her presentation as a "big success" and the outcome was that she was able to post the RFP. She explains, "It wasn't just the way I presented it but also the way I anticipated all of their questions. There weren't any things that I felt I left out." What, we asked, would she say was the key to a successful presentation? She responded, "The key to success was the research part. I study a lot; I learn my stuff before I go and, while I don't know everything, I know a lot. I do research; I especially try to look more into the technical side and if I don't understand it too much I'll go and talk to one of our engineers and ask him to explain it to me. Getting information together is a team effort. I talk to different people, they sit down and talk to me. Any questions I have I can email them or call them. I wasn't reticent about my presentation because I knew the research. I knew what I was saying."

We'd say the research Alice did as she selected and organized her content for presentation also accounted for Alice's confidence in her presentation ability. This confidence, in turn, was projected to her audience, enhancing her credibility and expertise and contributing to her presentation success.

Research at DD Inc.

Deborah Garcia, President and CEO of Digital Denim, Inc. has heard rumors that a new technology will soon be introduced that promises to revolutionize the online fashion industry. She calls in Jacqueline Cooper, Director of Information Technology (IT) at DD Inc., and asks her to see if she can find out any additional information about what she has heard. She asks Jacqueline to send the information to her as quickly as possible in an e-memo.

Jacqueline considers the range of resources available to her to find the information Deborah needs. She sets about her task.

Learning Check

1. What is information literacy?
2. Name three information problem-solving models.
3. How is Kuhlthau's model different from the others?
4. What did Kuhlthau's research reveal about how we conduct the research process?
5. What are the eight general research skills for information literacy?

Do & Discuss

Jacqueline Cooper has been given a research task to locate information about any new technologies developed that may enhance DD Inc.'s Web site presence. Help Jacqueline accomplish her task by answering the following questions:

*   Since her research task has been clearly defined by Deborah, what is the first thing Jacqueline must do as she begins her research task?
*   What other steps must Jacqueline take to accomplish her research goal?
*   What are some sources Jacqueline might use to find information on her research topic?
*   Although Deborah has asked for Jacqueline's information to be presented in the form of an email memo, what other decisions must Jacqueline make about the way her information is presented?

While researching, selecting, and organizing your content, it's almost impossible not to also be thinking about your technique, the delivery method(s) you will use to present your content to your audience. The next three chapters of this book describe the major techniques for presenting information, written, oral, and multimedia. We begin with written presentations in chapter 7.

Notes

1. Michael Eisenberg and Robert E. Berkowitz, *Information Problem-Solving: The Big Six Skills Approach to Library and Information Skills Instruction* (Norwood, N.J.: Ablex, 1990).
2. Barbara Stripling and Judy M. Pitts, *Brainstorms and Blueprints.* (Englewood, Colo.: Libraries Unlimited, 1988).
3. Carol Kuhlthau, "Inside the Search Process: Information Seeking from the User's Perspective," *Journal of the American Society of Information Science* 42, no. 5 (1991): 361-371.
4. Carol Kuhlthau, "Implementing a Process Approach to Information Skills: A Study Identifying Indicators of Success in Library Media Programs," *School Library Media Quarterly* 22, no.1 (1993): 11-18.
5. Ruth V. Small and Marilyn P. Arnone, *Turning Kids On to Research: The Power of Motivation* (Englewood, Colo.: Libraries Unlimited, 2000).

Source of Quote

American Association of School Librarians and Association for Educational Communications and Technology. *Information Power: Building Partnerships for Learning.* Chicago: American Library Association, 1998.

Chapter 7

T Is for Technique:
Written Presentations

PACT Model©

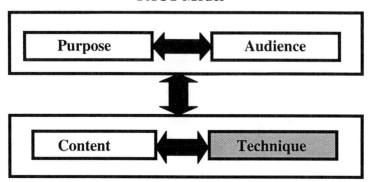

This chapter is about written presentations, the first of three chapters in this book related to the "T" in the PACT Model: Technique. Technique refers to the presentation modes, formats, and strategies we select to deliver a presentation to our audience.

Often, we don't think of written documents as presentations—but, of course, they are. Every time we communicate with someone else, no matter what the delivery method, we are creating a form of presentation.

Written presentations can have any of the four purposes. For example a flyer may be used to inform, a newsletter to influence, a poster to inspire, or a training manual to instruct. Some written presentations are intended as messages "inside the bottle"; that is, communication that is intended for an audience inside the organization (e.g., memos). Others are directed toward an audience "outside the bottle," that are external to the organization (e.g., business letters). Still others may be intended for either internal or external audiences (e.g., annual reports).

The content of written presentations may use any of the organizational structures. Some, such as memos and executive summaries, are brief, focusing on core information, while others, such as annual reports, often include both clarifying and enriching information.

We often think of written presentations as literally written on paper or some other form of writing surface. However with the technologies currently available, more and more traditionally paper-based (hard copy) presentations are delivered in electronic form. If produced in hard copy, they must be developed and reviewed carefully as, once delivered, they cannot be changed (like the company poster with the wrong contact information that we described earlier).

In this chapter, we use the term "written" to encompass text-intensive presentations using a variety of formats. As you proceed through the chapter and subsequent technique chapters, keep in mind each of the other parts of PACT and their impact on the type of techniques you choose for your presentations.

> *If you would not be forgotten, as soon as you are dead and rotten, either write things worth reading, or do things worth the writing.*
>
> Benjamin Franklin, *Poor Richard's Almanack*

Objectives

By the end of chapter 7, you should be able to:

- Identify written presentations that can be internal, external, or either internal or external,
- describe essential presentation factors unique to internal and external presentations,
- understand the difference between an abstract and an annotation, and
- recognize some of the value-added factors that must be addressed when writing a resume.

Messages Inside the Bottle

We begin with examples of written messages that are in-tended strictly for *internal* consumption; that is, to be delivered to one or more audiences within an organization. These include memos and job aids.

Memos

Internal communications, when not spoken, often take the form of a memorandum (a.k.a. memo). Memos are among the most common forms of business communications. While they are, in general, informal notes to one or more people within the organization that focus on a single topic (e.g., a decision that has been made, an announcement) and are brief in nature (often no longer than one or two paragraphs), they can be important and powerful. Many organizations depend on memos for their everyday communication. Memos often play a key role in making sure that members of an organization remain aware of important events and decisions.

Memos typically use a standard, recognizable format containing the following core information elements: the current date, to whom the memo is addressed, from whom the memo originates, and the overall subject of the memo (often abbreviated with RE for Regarding or Subject, followed by a colon. In order to add a personal touch and to verify that the message of the memo has been approved, the sender typically signs or initials the memo (electronic memos may include this as well).[1]

Most importantly, memos need to be brief (long enough to convey the message) and clear (of purpose and content). They should be self-contained (consisting of the critical core information) so that people who read them will not need to look elsewhere or ask for further details or clarification. Nothing detracts from a memo more than unnecessary or unclear information (noise). For example, a memo announcing a meeting should include when and where the meeting will be held, who should attend, the purpose of the meeting, what attendees will be expected to do at the meeting, and what, if anything, they need to do to prepare. Sometimes, supplementary presentations like the meeting agenda or preparatory readings are attached.

The tone of the memo should be friendly and relatively informal rather than formal and austere. In many organizations, there is a specialized jargon or a set of commonly used technical terms. You can include these terms in memos that you know are only intended for employees or organization members familiar with them. If you think a technical term or jargon-laden phrase has any chance of confusing your audience, opt for a more common word term or phrase. Value-added factors like simplicity, noise reduction, and consistent formatting are essential to memos.

> ### *Think About*
> Think of a memo you received. Was it brief and to the point? Did it have all of the core information required for understanding? Did it include any unnecessary information?

While paper-based memos typed or handwritten on letterhead or special memo pads are still used in some organizations, more often in today's digital world memos are delivered in electronic form via an internal intranet or email system. The format of most e-memos is, in fact, very similar to most memos.

Flashback

Remember the e-memo Deborah Garcia sent to her management team in chapter 2? There was a header that told who sent the message, to whom it was addressed, the subject, and the date. Using email to present a memo made the process of distribution easier, but be careful. The culture of an organization or company may assign different values to paper and electronic communications. In some organizations, communications on paper may seem more important, while in others email or a similar electronic format may be preferred.

Look at the paper-based memo below. See if you can identify all of the critical elements. In terms of PACT, what is the purpose of this written presentation? Who is the intended audience? What is the main topic of the content? You can see how even a brief presentation such as a memo can and should address all of the PACT components. (By the way, did you notice the logo and slogan?)

Small Press Publishers, Inc.
297 Center Street
Syracuse, New York 13011

<u>MEMO</u>

Date: January 18, 2001
To: Ella Small, President & CEO
From: William Johnstone, Marketing Director
Re: Brochures

The new marketing brochures have been printed and are about to be mailed out to 10,000 bookstores throughout the United States. It is anticipated that the brochures will translate into millions of new customers for our latest publications, particularly the mystery series by Agatha King and the science fiction series by our newest Pulitzer Prize-winning author, Steven Christie. I will continue to keep you informed as to the results of this new marketing effort.

"Small Press, Large Value"

Job Aids

Have you ever been in a restaurant and noticed a poster displaying the correct way to perform the Heimlich Maneuver on a choking victim? Have you ever seen a template that fits over a keyboard to help you remember the commands in a computer program? Do you use an electronic email address book to keep track of those people to whom you frequently send messages? Do you remember the list of research skills and sub-skills we included in chapter 6? These are all examples of *job aids*.

A job aid's purpose is typically as an instructing presentation that helps a person remember already learned information or processes to support work performance or other activities. Job aids serve as performance support tools and are used when the need arises. For example, you could use our job aid on research skills and sub-skills the next time you have a research project or are researching information for your next presentation.

Job aids save an organization both time and money by reducing the need for additional teaching or training. Job aids are most useful when:

- the information or task is complex and/or long,
- time and/or safety is critical,
- the task is simple and performed infrequently,
- the rules or content changes frequently,
- there is heavy job turnover, or
- the individual is not expected to be an expert but must perform the task quickly without the benefit of more detailed directions.[2]

The intended audience for a job aid is anyone who must remember specific information or perform a given task or process. The content of a job aid may be organized using any of the TOP ACT organizational schemes. The choking victim poster organizes information by time, showing the steps to be taken in sequential order. The keyboard template organizes by topic related to each key command. The email address book organizes information in alphabetical order for easy access to and location of needed information.

Job aids consist mainly of core information but may have illustrations or other clarifying information. Quality, noise reduction, and ease of use are important value-added factors to consider in the development of job aids. They can take almost any form—from paper-based help sheets to plastic templates to cardboard posters to electronic help mechanisms. We've even seen job aids developed as mouse pads, rulers, hanging mobiles, and frames that fit onto a computer monitor. The only limitation is your own imagination (and the job aid's purpose, audience, and content).

To this point, you've been reading about formats primarily used to communicate with people internal to your organization. Now, let's look at some written presentations intended for *external* audiences.

Messages Outside the Bottle

External written presentations are critical communication for any organization. They may be the primary and initial communication delivered to your clients, customers, or potential employer.

Business Cards

You've probably never thought of a business card as a type of presentation. In fact, it is every bit as much of a written presentation as a report or speech. It is often the first presentation you make as a representative of your organization and it can convey a powerful message to and lasting impression on your audience.

Like all other presentations, a business card should reflect each of the PACT components. The purpose is to inform your audience, providing a way for others to remember essential information about you. Your audience could be colleagues, customers, competitors, or even prospective employers.

While the amount of space is very limited on a business card, there is some core information that is required such as your name, organization, and contact information (typically, address, phone number, fax number, and email address).

While it's unlikely that your card will include any clarifying information, you may want to include enriching information such as a company logo and/or slogan. Noise reduction is essential.

In terms of technique, you want to make your business card memorable and a "keeper." The typeface, background color, font color, and even the card stock you use can contribute to your message. Look at the two business cards below for DD Inc.'s President, Deborah Garcia. What message do you think each conveys?

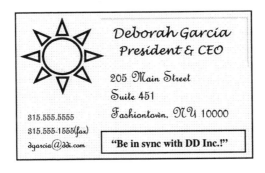

Deborah Garcia
President & CEO

205 Main Street
Suite 451
Fashiontown, NY 10000

315.555.5555
315.555-1555(fax)
dgarcia@ddi.com

"Be in sync with DD Inc.!"

"Be in sync
with DD Inc.!"

Deborah Garcia
President & CEO
Digital Denim, Inc.

205 Main Street   315.555.5555
Suite 451   315.555.1555(fax)
Fashiontown. NY 10000   daarcia@ddi.com

Here are some important rules-of-thumb for business cards (and any written presentation):

- The eye should be led to the most important information first by using boldface and a larger font size.
- The reader's attention should proceed from left to right, top to bottom.
- The font should be sans serif (simple, without "curly-q's") so that it is clear and easy to read. Examples of sans serif fonts are Arial, Geneva, and Tahoma.
- If a background color (other than white or ivory) is used, it should be a light neutral color (gray or buff) so the color doesn't distract from the information.
- Bold typeface should be used sparingly.
- Avoid a cluttered look where one piece of information appears to be "fighting" with another.

While the second card follows these rules, the first card violates almost all of them. You can probably imagine what kind of impression Deborah would make on prospective clients if she used that card! (It must be noted, however, that some companies that are in creative fields might want their cards and logos to "break the mold"; that is, sometimes a bold background or artistic brush stroke can help to make a statement and reinforce credibility for a person from the arts (e.g., a sculptor, a video producer, an interior designer).

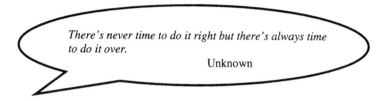

There's never time to do it right but there's always time to do it over.

Unknown

Business Letters

A letter communicates more than just content. Its format indicates whether it is intended to convey business, personal, or some other type of information. Quality factors communicate whether the presenter cares about his or her message. A letter filled with grammatical, spelling, or typing errors, out-of-date, disorganized, or omission of critical information sends a negative message, regardless of the importance of the topic.

A business letter should contain the following:

- Letterhead/organization logo/address
- Date of creation
- Address of intended receiver exactly as it will appear on the envelope
- Salutation (e.g., "Dear Ms.___:" or "Dear Sir:" or "ATTENTION: Marketing Department" if it's an organization)
- Message (or Body) of letter
- Closing (e.g., "Sincerely,")
- Signature block (presenter's name and title)
- Reference initials (presenter's initials in caps; if typed by someone else they should be followed by a colon and the typist's initials in lower case)
- Enclosure indicator (abbreviated "Enc") if something else is to be included
- "PC" or "CC" notation (if anyone will be sent a personal or courtesy copy)[3]

Brochures

Brochures are often used as marketing tools for an organization. Their purpose is always to inform but can sometimes also be used to inspire, influence, or instruct. The audience for a brochure can be as narrow as a specific group or as wide as the general public. The content is typically a combination of core, clarifying, and enriching information elements, with the latter often consisting of graphics, photos, or quotes (e.g., testimonials). Quality and ease of use are essential value-added factors for brochures.

While brochures can be highly sophisticated or unusual in style, form, or size, many quality brochures are still paper-based on 8 ½" x 11" paper folded lengthwise in thirds (called a *trifold*) with each of the six panels (front and back) containing distinct information. The first panel usually contains content that identifies the topic (and sometimes intended audience) of the brochure. The back of the brochure (which is actually the fifth panel) often contains mailing information, if the brochure is to be mailed without an envelope. Most often, content is printed vertically on each panel and is organized by topic (although some are printed horizontally and can use any of the organizational schemes).

Effective brochures often contain graphics or photographs as enriching information and make them more attractive. Unless delivered directly to the intended audience through the mail or in person, it is important to make them as appealing as possible so that people will pick them up and read them (sometimes your brochure may be sitting on a table or in a display rack competing with many others so you will need to find ways to make yours stand out from the rest). Desktop publishing programs make creating simple but elegant brochures a snap, even if you are not a graphic designer by trade!

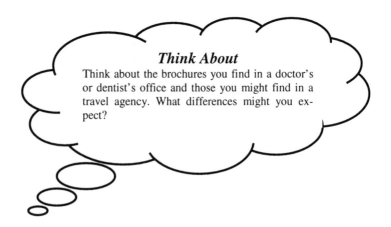

Think About

Think about the brochures you find in a doctor's or dentist's office and those you might find in a travel agency. What differences might you expect?

Messages That Can Go Either Way

There are written presentations that are intended for internal and/or external audiences. For example, your CEO may want to take the same information you have presented in a brochure for a handout, organizing the information differently, emphasizing different topics, or presenting information in different amounts and scope to different audiences (e.g., the company's employees versus the company's stockholders). He may use the same handout for both groups or completely different ones.

Here's another example. The Dean may want to send the college's newsletter to both internal constituents (faculty, students, staff) and external constituents (alumni, potential donors). Some examples of presentations that can be presented internally or externally are resumes, handouts, abstracts, executive summaries, newsletters, and annual reports.

> *The closest most people ever come to reaching their ideal is when they write their resumes.*
>   Anonymous

Resumes

When you create a resume, you are preparing to present *yourself* to a potential employer or other audience. Resumes require a great deal of information in a small amount of space. Often, your resume is the first (and hopefully not the last) impression that an employer has of you. Your ability to organize, summarize and present your relevant work experience, educational background, and special qualifications is a direct reflection on you and your potential employability. While resumes often go to external audiences, they may also be required for presentation within your own organization (e.g., for promotion, a workshop for another unit), particularly if it is a large organization like a government agency, university, or large corporation.

As with other types of presentations, it is essential to consider the purpose of the resume and its accompanying cover letter (more about cover letters later). Is it intended to land a new job, reenter the job market, change careers, get a promotion at a current job, or support your credentials? Is your audience a potential employer, your current boss, or your work team? The resume is used to inform but the cover letter must inspire the reader to review your resume and motivate him or her to select you over other applicants.

Once you have identified your purpose and audience, you must think about how to organize and select the content you will include.

Remember TOP ACT? These are as useful for organizing a resume as any other type of presentation. Most resumes are organized first and foremost by topic, such as work experience and educational background. Other topics to include are specific to the individual; for example, a college professor might include publications and service activities within his or her institution or professional community. A corporate executive might include information about involvement in community activities and consulting experiences. An IT manager might include technology expertise and special projects on which he or she has worked.

Within the topic organization, the resume often uses a time (or chronological) and continuum order to specify each item within that topic. For example, you would likely list your work experience in temporal order, beginning with the most recent job you have held, but you typically would list your educational background by specifying degrees from highest (e.g., master's degree) to lowest (high school diploma) achieved (which does not always follow a time order).

The content you select will come from two major sources. First, you will need to perform a type of self-assessment (e.g., individual brainstorming) in which you identify your skills and areas of expertise, achievements and major responsibilities, and any personal characteristics that highlight special qualities that make you highly desirable for employment (e.g., perseverance, high motivation).

Content selection will also require you to conduct research, using both print and electronic sources to gather information about your specific career field such as characteristics of the work environment, potential for career advancement, and location and type of job opportunities.

Resumes typically consist of mostly factual core information including:

- name, address, phone number (including the area code), and email address on the top of the first page,
- work experience, periods of employment, and job titles, and
- education, dates of graduation, degrees, majors.

You may also include clarifying information, such as an explanation of the types of responsibilities that you assumed in a particular job or related experience or a list of your areas of expertise (e.g., Web design skills), and enriching information such as a statement of your career goal, relevant personal characteristics, language proficiency, honors or awards, military service, professional affiliations or memberships, credentials or licenses and any other relevant experiences that enhance credentials (e.g., in-service training).

The amount and scope of information to include in a resume depend upon the breadth and amount of background and experience you have had. It must be long enough to cover all relevant information but brief enough so as not to bore a potential employer. Many business employers prefer resumes of no more than two pages in length while college employers often place no limit on the length of a prospective faculty or administrator's resume.

An effective resume addresses most, if not all, of Taylor's value-added factors. First, it's important to consider quality issues including information that is correct (free of typos, grammatical errors, etc.), complete (all essential information), current (updated regularly), and credible (information that exemplifies your knowledge and expertise).

At times, your resume will be targeted to a very specific audience, sometimes even one individual. This means that it must be flexible enough so that it is adaptable to varying audiences; i.e., you are able to organize and select content that specifically highlights those achievements, experiences, and capabilities that address the precise needs of a given audience. For example, if there is a specific job that you have targeted to pursue, you might want to include information that would have an impact on your prospective employer that you wouldn't include in a general resume used to blanket the market.

Finally, your content should be organized neatly in a way that facilitates ease of use and time-savings, utilizing a standardized format with consistent headings, underlines, italics, bullet points, indentations, capital letters, etc. and within the page limit, if specified.

Let's look at an example. Here is the two-page resume of a fictional college graduate, Ima Presenter, submitted when she applied for her first job. Notice how Ima used action words such as "created," "supervised," "developed," and "monitored" to describe each of her accomplished tasks. Also, notice how what might seem like mundane or unimportant tasks performed in a summer job or part-time job can actually be an important contribution to your overall qualifications. For example, while Ima's job at an automobile towing service during her summer break from college may have seemed unrelated to her career goals, she was able to include some of her activities that were actually highly relevant, such as developing a local area network, delivering training, and creating a job aid. As you prepare your resume, make a list of everything you did (even the smallest tasks) for each experience. Most likely, you will find relevant information to include in your resume that provides a clearer and broader picture of your skills and knowledge.

Ima Presenter
119 Main Street
Candlewood, New York 13001
315/555-5555
Ipresent@netway.com

CAREER GOAL: To manage information systems for an Internet start-up company.

EDUCATION
* Southwestern University, College of Information and Technology, Azure, Arizona, Bachelor of Science in Information Management and Technology, May 2000.

TECHNICAL SKILLS
* Operating Systems: Windows, UNIX, PC, Macintosh
* Programming Languages: Pascal, Basic, Perl, HTML, Java, C++
* Software: MS Office, Adobe Photoshop, PageMaker, FileMaker Pro,
* Networking abilities for Local and Wide Area Networks

RELEVANT COURSEWORK
* Information Analysis of Organizational Systems
* Information Consultation
* Telecommunications Regulations
* Database Management
* Information Reporting and Presentation

PROJECTS
* Project Analysis and Internship at the United Charities of Central New York
    o Researched and evaluated current and proposed computer network infrastructure
    o Prepared and presented report summarizing findings including recommendations, costs, implementation scenarios, and alternatives
* Team Project Analysis of Candlewood School District's Computing System
* Developed survey tool for analysis and information-gathering stage of project

RELEVANT WORK EXPERIENCE
Web Site Designer   *Fall 1996-Present*
Office of Career Planning, Southwestern University, Glenson, AZ
- Created home pages and resumes for a diverse student population so that information is available online for greater visibility.
- Developed original designs and graphics to more effectively illustrate students' qualifications.

Computer Analyst   *May-September 1996*
Jack's Tow Service, Candlewood, NY
- Developed a Local Area Network linking Jack's Tow Service to Joe's Auto Body in order to improve communications between the two locations.
- Trained employees to better utilize and update the network.
- Created job aid for utilizing and updating network.

OTHER WORK EXPERIENCE
Technical Intern   *September-May 1996*
Belen Widget Technology, Bloomfield, MI
- Monitored $500,000 of inventory using Excel.
- Responsible for meeting weekly quotas in sales and expenditures.
- Supervised employees in widget assembly department.
- Ensured that quality control standards were maintained on each widget before shipping.

PERSONAL INTERESTS
Hobbies: Reading, mountain climbing, traveling.

REFERENCES
Available upon request.

> **Think About**
>
> When you create a written presentation, do you think carefully about the words you use. Do you use "power" words (words that have impact, gain attention, evoke emotion, etc.) rather than more neutral ones, where appropriate? Use a dictionary or thesaurus to help you find just the right power words for your presentation.

The Cover Letter

A cover letter is a type of business letter that explains an enclosure such as a resume or report addressed to a specific audience. Its main purpose is to influence, i.e., to encourage the target audience to read the attachment. Ima's cover letter accompanied her resume which was sent both electronically and in paper form (printed on high-quality bond paper in a subtle grey tone) to several companies. In it, she introduced herself, described the type of job she was seeking, described briefly why she was well qualified for a position with their organization, and requested an interview. Ima's cover letter and resume were successful information presentations—she got an interview and the job!

Handouts

Handouts are most often used to highlight or supplement some other larger type of presentation, such as an oral or multimedia presentation. The decision whether or not to have handouts depends on the purpose, audience, content, and technique of that larger presentation.

—Presentation Tip—
Your handout should include the title and date of the presentation and the presenter's name and organization somewhere on the handout.

The purpose of a handout is (1) generally to inform, although it could be used for other purposes as well and (2) to provide a structure of the information presented (serving as a presentation guide for both presenter and audience). The content in a handout may provide a brief outline or summary of the core information in a larger presentation or may provide additional information, clarifying information if the core presentation is complex or difficult to understand, and/or enriching information if there is information you want your audience to have but do not intend to include it in your oral presentation. For example, if the presentation is an oral presentation accompanied by PowerPoint slides, the presenter may give the audience a handout that contains the slides themselves, a list of references used to construct the presentation, or an in-depth description of a concept only briefly addressed in the oral presentation. Noise reduction is the most critical value-added factor for handouts.

—Presentation Tip—
Never put your entire presentation in a handout. Your audience will begin to wonder why they need you at all!

Once you've decided to provide a handout, when do you distribute it to your audience? If you want your audience to follow along with you or if some members of your audience will have a hard time seeing your presentation because they are sitting in the back of a large auditorium or meeting hall, it would be appropriate to provide the handout at the beginning of your presentation. However, if neither is the case, you have to carefully consider the possibility that your audience will focus on the handout (rather than what you are saying, showing, or demonstrating) if you hand it out too early. Furthermore, some of your audience members could begin shuffling and turning pages (or worse, using the handout as a fan!), which is likely to be highly distracting to both yourself and others in the audience.

Often, distributing the handout at the end (and announcing you will do that early in your presentation) can be the most effective use of the handout, especially if the content is intended as review or enrichment. Still another alternative when you have a series of handouts is to distribute each piece at the time you are about to cover the particular topic that the handout addresses.

Some experts suggest having handouts professionally produced. With the simplicity and quality of today's presentation and desktop publishing software, we think it is easier than ever to produce your own professional-looking handouts. If your handout is more than one page, or if you are giving out more than one handout, you might want to consider grouping them within some type of folder for ease of use (you might want to include some blank paper for note-taking as well).

Here's another idea for handouts. Rather than giving all of the information you intend to provide, include some blanks where information is purposely omitted. Then you and your audience fill in the blanks as you present that information. This is a great way to keep your audience's attention and promote their active involvement in your presentation. This works well with other types of presentations as well, such as videos and multimedia.

Handouts are typically textual (they can also contain visual information) and paper-based (although they could be in electronic or other form) so that you leave your audience with something tangible in hand. This emphasizes the importance of your handout as a presentation of its own. It also provides a reference for future use by your audience. Make sure there is up-to-date contact information on your handouts as they can often serve as referrals for consulting or requests for additional presentations.

Think About

Think about an excellent oral presentation that you attended. Was there a handout? If so, did it reinforce the importance and usefulness of the presentation? If not, did you feel dissatisfied with the presentation?

Saying a Lot with Few Words

Often it is necessary to take a large amount of information and reduce it to a few words. For example, you are preparing an article for the company newsletter on a topic that synthesizes information covered in one or more other reports. You have very little room to capture the essence of those other reports. You need to *abstract* the information; that is, present it in a brief and succinct format. Or say you've just completed your annual report to the CEO and it's 150 pages long. The CEO is about to go into a meeting with the Board of Directors and has to give them a summary of what the report reveals. Most likely, the CEO will ask you to prepare an *executive summary*, a brief overview of the most important points of the report that can be shared with the board. In the next section of this chapter, we describe abstracts and executive summaries and how to create them, after which we discuss their larger counterparts, newsletters and annual reports.

Abstracts and executive summaries serve a simple and powerful purpose. They take a large amount of information and hone it down to the essentials. They allow the reader to make decisions about information contained in a document or group of documents without having to read all of the content in that document. At a time when many people feel overwhelmed by the amount of information available to them, this can be a vitally important function.

Abstracts

An abstract provides an abbreviated representation of a larger presentation, reflecting its purpose and retaining its essential ideas in a brief format. Abstracts retain a neutral tone, summarizing information in the larger document with appropriate emphases, without interpretation or criticism.[4]

There are two basic types of abstract: informative and indicative. Informative abstracts condense the essential ideas of the original document, and attempt to relate those ideas from the point of view of the document's author. An indicative abstract serves as a guide to a written document, but it is written from the perspective of an informed but impartial reader.[5]

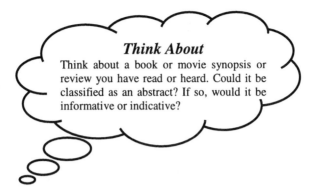

Think About

Think about a book or movie synopsis or review you have read or heard. Could it be classified as an abstract? If so, would it be informative or indicative?

Abstracts need to be distinguished from annotations. Annotations are typically very short, fifty words or less. They are used in bibliographies and some databases to describe documents. Though they are related to abstracts, they contain less information and may contain opinions regarding the document's usefulness or quality.

Here's a hypothetical example of an annotation for a book about annotations.

Annot, A.T. (1996). Writing annotations. *Journal of Document Annotations.* 26 *(2)*:187-195.

I got all the facts about writing annotations and several different examples from this source. The author is very readable and includes a detailed annotated bibliography.

While annotations provide a simple expression of a document's content, an abstract goes beyond the content and tries to reflect the character of the document. Someone writing an abstract is typically trying to summarize information written by someone else. Because of this, the abstract creator should strive to be neutral, accurately reflecting what the author or authors said, without editorializing.

An abstract should capture the essential ideas of a document. If a document presents multiple ideas, give those ideas the same weight they receive in the original document. If a topic is mentioned briefly, it should not be given a great deal of attention. If it is not central, it does not necessarily need to appear in an abstract. This is another judgment call, but always try to preserve the importance ideas were given by the original author.

Here's an example of an abstract that appears in the online database of the U.S. Department of Education's Educational Resources Information Center (ERIC). It is the abstract for a document about abstracting entitled *The Art of Abstracting* by Edward T. Cremmins.[5]

ABSTRACT: A three-stage analytical reading method for the composition of informative and indicative abstracts by authors and abstractors is presented in this monograph, along with background information on the abstracting process and a discussion of professional considerations in abstracting. An introduction to abstracts and abstracting precedes general advice for abstractors and a summary of the processes of human and computer-assisted abstracting and translating. Sections on retrieval reading, creative reading, and critical reading comprise the proposed three-stage method for abstracting, with rules and examples provided for each stage. The importance of analytical reading in the writing of good-quality abstracts, the length and style of abstracts, the time required for writing abstracts, and the function of thinking and cognition skills within abstracting and other information-processing activities are described. A syntopical index to the literature on abstracting style is also included. The interrelationships between abstractors, readers, information scientists, managers or sponsors of abstracting services, and editors or reviewers of abstracts are examined, as are the topics of abstracting as a profession and the professional status of abstractors. A glossary, seven appendices including annotated bibliographies and further rules and examples for abstracting, a list of 37 references, and an index conclude the publication.

Because the audience for an abstract has typically not read the document or documents being summarized, you need to keep their needs foremost in mind. For what purpose do they need the information in the document? Will they use the abstract without reading the original document, or will they use the abstract to decide whether they want to read the original document? What prior experience do they have with the subject? Will they need to have additional explanation (e.g., technical terms) or will they find the abstract easy to understand on their own? When writing an abstract, never underestimate the power of just asking one or more members of your target audience what they need. Most people are glad to tell you what they want. Asking that kind of question makes you look more professional, and it increases the chances that your abstract will be useful.

There are also some technical tips to keep in mind when writing abstracts. These tips can help avoid confusion:

- When using acronyms, include a written-out version in parentheses.
- Avoid abbreviations; write out the word or phrase.
- Don't use evaluative language unless clearly identified as yours and not that of the original author.
- Use complete sentences (proper grammar, spelling, and punctuation).
- Provide proper references to the original presentation.

Executive Summaries

While abstracts are typically used to summarize journal articles and research reports, executive summaries are most often used in organizations to summarize in-depth reports. Executive summaries are intended for an audience (e.g., your boss) who often has neither the time nor the patience to read a lengthy report but who wants to read a quick summary of key points to decide if he or she should read the entire report. If you know exactly who your audience is, you may want to tailor your executive summary to that audience. Different audiences may require different amounts, types, or organization of content.

Executive summaries are typically one to two pages in length and provide a clear, concise, and readable overview of all of the significant points, important decisions, major conclusions and recommendations and other essential core information covered in the larger presentation. Like abstracts, they are free of personal opinions, capture the essence of the larger presentation by including only core information elements, and can stand on their own as presentations themselves. They are typically free of jargon and technical terms that may have been explained in the larger report, substituting simpler, more familiar terms. Both abstracts and executive summaries emphasize noise reduction as their primary value-added factor.

Here are some basic steps that you can follow in preparing an abstract or executive summary:

1. Read the article or report from beginning to end to get a general sense of what it says.
2. Go back and read it again, underlining/highlighting/listing the major points of importance.
3. Rewrite these points as briefly and clearly as possible.

Writing an effective abstract or executive summary can be a challenge, but it is worth the effort. The general rules and basic steps specified above should facilitate and enable you to become comfortable with the process.

Newsletters

Newsletters are somewhat informal in tone and largely informing in purpose, but may include messages that inspire readers, as well. While often internal to an organization, newsletters may also serve as a way of communicating current events and issues to constituencies outside the organization as well. For example, a professional organization's newsletter may also provide useful information to those who are interested in some issues but are not members of the organization.

Unless there are only one or two topics comprising the content of a newsletter, the amount of information on any one topic is necessarily brief due to space limitations. Most, if not all, information has a direct relationship to the organization producing the newsletter. All three types of information elements (core, clarifying, enriching) may be found in newsletters, and they typically use a topical organizational structure with headings and subheadings separating topics. In terms of value-added factors, the emphasis in newsletters is on content that is current, simple, and browsable. Content may include visual and numerical content forms like tables or charts for clarification and cartoons and attention-focusing devices like boxes and arrows for enrichment.

—Presentation Tip—

With any type of visual, always try to include a caption both for clarity and to capture the audience's attention.

Newsletters can be paper-based or in electronic form (i.e., e-newsletters) and typically take one of two formats. They either are typed straight across a page or have two or three columns. Newsletters use headings to separate topics. A consistent layout improves ease of use. They usually have a banner across the top of the front page that includes the organization, date of publication, and other identifying information. There are several easy-to-use desktop publishing packages available today that allow you to create professional-looking newsletters, brochures, business cards, business letterhead stationery, and other types of written presentations relatively quickly.

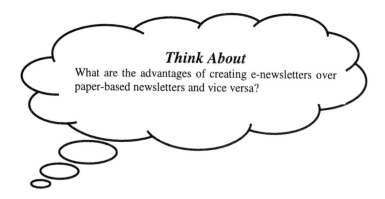

Think About

What are the advantages of creating e-newsletters over paper-based newsletters and vice versa?

Annual Reports

Annual reports are often meant as internal documents that help in organizational planning and decision-making. They contain large amounts of information presented and may summarize the work of a single person, a department or other unit, or an entire organization over the period of a year.

Because of this variability in scope, annual reports come in many forms. An annual report for an entire company might be hundreds of pages long and many people might contribute to it. An annual report written by a student to describe his or her own learning progress might be very brief. While this variety makes it difficult to generalize too broadly, some rules of thumb apply to almost any annual report.

Like an abstract, an annual report should be written in an objective tone. If, for example, you are writing a report on your own work, don't be afraid to take credit for (without bragging about) your accomplishments. A modest description often will impress people more than a boastful one. At the same time, do not try to hide any problems. Talk about them and focus on what you are currently doing or plan to do in order to solve them. Everyone runs into problems periodically, and the more you look like a problem solver, the more you are likely to convince people you can be effective.

As with all the forms of communication described in this book, remember your audience and its purpose. Will the report be used to make budget decisions? If so, include clear, relevant financial information. Will it be used to make decisions as to grades, salary increases, or promotions? In that case be clear about a person's achievements and shortcomings and how their skills and knowledge fit the goals of the larger organization. Will it be used to inform investors of the com-

pany's activities and progress? The annual report is a good technique
for presenting this kind of big picture.

The content of an annual report typically uses one of two types of
organization. It either reviews the year's accomplishments by topic or
provides a temporal (time) structure that chronicles those accomplishments through the year.

Quality is the most critical value-added factor (all four Cs) for annual reports. It is essential that the report is correct in every detail, that
it is current and up-to-date, that it is complete in its coverage of all areas of interest, and that the information itself is credible and is derived
from credible sources. Some annual reports demand the filtering of any
noise that could distract or annoy the reader. Including a detailed table
of contents and providing a consistent layout and use of headings facilitate ease of use (these organizational tools are also useful in stand-alone
multimedia and Web site design as you will learn in chapter 9). Annual
reports often contain visual (e.g., photographs, floor plans) and numerical (e.g., financial charts, employment graphs) content forms as clarifying and enriching information elements.

Let's Hear It! ◁))

When Donna Callahan was asked to go to Cary, North Carolina, to interview for the position of Marketing Strategist at SAS, the largest pri-
vately held business-intelligence software and services company in the
world, she was told she had to prepare and deliver two presentations as
part of the interview process. What's more, she was provided with two
scenarios that required her to come up with a strategy for a telecommunications churn solution. The only problem was that Donna was not
familiar with churn management! (Neither were we, so Donna explained that churn is when customers are switching from one telecommunications provider to another.) Churn management is the effort to try
to keep that from happening by understanding these behaviors and predicting who is likely to churn in the future. Churn management is an
important element of the SAS Solution for Customer Relationship
Management (or CRM).

Donna discovered that her audience would consist of two managers and four staff members of the Strategic Marketing Group at SAS.
She was given the two scenarios in advance and had about two weeks
to prepare. "That was good because I had to understand not only the
technology and terms they were using but how the technology solves
their customer's problems. I had to do a lot of investigating about

SAS's products and software because I had never worked with them," Donna told us. "I did have several years of business experience at IBM, GE, and utility companies working in Marketing and Sales, Customer Service, and field programs developing and implementing customer information systems." The experience would later come in very handy in her presentations, as her unique enterprise wide perspective was valuable to her audience.

The scenarios required Donna to deliver a presentation within her presentation. In the first scenario, Donna was supposed to be presenting to a churn management committee. The purpose of the presentation was to position the value of working with SAS in order to provide a solution and partner in its development. Donna organized her content by topics; deciding to begin with a brief overview of telecommunications churn, then presenting a solution that she had envisioned and the strategy for achieving that vision, telling something about SAS's current churn solution, and ending with a pitch about the value of partnering.

In the second scenario, Donna's presentation was supposed to be delivered to SAS's development team. The purpose of the second presentation was to explain why SAS should invest resources to build such an application. Donna again used a topic organizational scheme, starting with a summary of the market and the need for a telecommunications churn management solution as her hook, then describing the different stages of churn management and providing some of the business problems that SAS might be able to solve during these different stages of churn.

The presentations were held in a large conference room with people seated around an oblong table. Donna stood at the front of the room. "I brought PowerPoint slides with me," Donna explains, "however when I got to the room, I found their projector didn't work! Luckily I had a back-up; I had brought paper copies of the PowerPoint slides with me, so I just went through them." She was limited to 10-15 minutes for each presentation with some time after each presentation for questions.

Obviously, Donna's presentations were successful; she got the job! Donna also found that there were some additional results. "After I finished, I knew I was successful when the audience asked me questions as though I was an expert in the field!" Donna continued. "I held their attention throughout each presentation; I was really into it! I was excited about my presentations, and my enthusiasm came across." We often observe that a presenter's enthusiasm is contagious to an audience.

We asked Donna to reflect on what she thought was the major contributing factor to her success and she came up with three factors!

"First of all, understanding my audience. I was presenting to people I had never met before. I found out in advance who would be at the presentation, what their roles in the company were, what their needs were, and what they might be looking for. I also knew another woman who worked inside SAS and I asked her send me any of their white papers. They had just completed a training class in Europe on churn in the telecommunications industry so she sent me information as well. Secondly, research was one of the key factors and it took time; it wasn't only the SAS products and solutions that I had to learn about, it was also about churn and the telecommunications. I had to learn the industry-specific business issues. Even if you understand the needs of the audience and provide value, if you didn't do the research and preparation, it wouldn't have been any good. Thirdly, I really had to focus on the purpose of that presentation constantly; I was always going back and saying, OK now, how does this refer back to what the purpose of the presentation is?" We have to agree with Donna that these three factors can certainly make or break a presentation!

What's Up at DD Inc.?

Dan Bernstein, Marketing Director at DDI Inc., thinks that DD Inc.'s marketing initiative should include direct mailings to DD Inc.'s actual and potential customers. He must first identify what groups comprise his target audience. Dan discovers that his primary audience is women between 15 and 25. His secondary audiences are women over 25 and men aged 15 and over. He then conducts survey and focus group research to determine the best and most cost-effective ways to reach his market.

In consultation with other officers of the company, Dan has decided to use the brochure as his marketing tool. He wants to design a brochure that is informative, yet will influence his audience to go to DD Inc.'s Web site. He wants the brochure to reflect the fun-loving, youthful image DD Inc. has worked so hard to create while, at the same time, portraying the company as a fiscally responsible, customer-centered business.

Learning Check

1. What is an example of a written presentation:

   a. intended for audiences internal to an organization?
   b. intended for audiences external to an organization?
   c. intended for audiences either internal or external to an organization?

2. What is a job aid?

3. What is the purpose of a cover letter?

4. What is considered the most critical value-added factor for handouts?

5. What is the difference between an abstract and an annotation?

Do & Discuss

Help Dan Bernstein design a brochure for DD Inc. using MS Publisher or other desktop publishing software. Consider:

- What information would you include?
- How would you organize your brochure?
- What non-text information would be useful?
- What would other officers in the company include in a brochure if they were designing it?

Deborah Garcia is in the process of writing DD Inc.'s annual report to its stockholders:

- What content should be included?
- Who should contribute to the writing of the report and why?

Find an article of interest from a newspaper or magazine. Write an abstract for the article that is no more than two paragraphs in length. In class, swap abstracts with another student and critique each other's abstract.

Find an example of a job aid. If possible, bring it to class or take a picture of it to share OR write a description of the job aid you found.

Create a checklist of items specific to the development of effective written presentations.

Coming Up...

Do your knees shake, your palms sweat, and your heart flutter just at the thought of making an oral presentation? While chapter 7 focused on written presentations, chapter 8 describes another form of presentation, one that strikes fear in the hearts of most people—the oral presentation. You'll find some techniques for overcoming anxiety along with other personal skills you can use for making powerful oral presentations in chapter 8.

Notes

1. Hank Staley, *Tongue & Quill: Your Practical (and Humorous) Guide to Better Communication* (Washington, D.C.: Pergamon-Brassey's International Defense Publishers, Inc., 1990), 135-137.
2. Allison Rossett and Jeannette Gautier-Downs, *The Handbook of Job Aids* (San Francisco: Pfeiffer & Company, 1991).
3. Staley, 129-131.
4. Section V: Cataloging, *ERIC Processing Manual* (Washington, D.C.: Educational Resources Information Center, U.S. Department of Education, June 1992), V13-16.
5. Edward T. Cremmins, *The Art of Abstracting*, ED224496 (Washington, D.C.: Educational Resources Information Center, U.S. Department of Education, 1982.

Chapter 8

T Is for Technique: Oral Presentations

PACT Model©

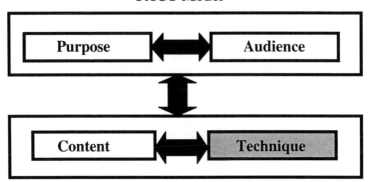

Why is presenting the Gettysburg Address in writing more effective than presenting Martin Luther King's *I Have a Dream* speech in writing? The answer is that we never saw Abraham Lincoln deliver the Gettysburg Address while we know that the impact of King's *I Have a Dream* speech was due to the combined power of his content and technique, his oral delivery. Once you have seen and heard Dr. King's address on video, reading it on paper just doesn't have the same effect. An oral presentation has the potential to go far beyond the words; it includes the voice, the gestures, the facial expressions, the media you use, etc.

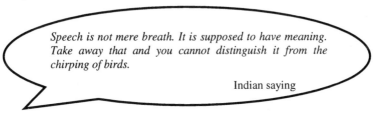

Speech is not mere breath. It is supposed to have meaning. Take away that and you cannot distinguish it from the chirping of birds.

Indian saying

As you begin to develop your personal oral presentation technique, focus on the various methods that help you effectively present information. In this chapter, you will learn some ways to present yourself and your content more effectively.

> ***Think About***
> One important medium you will use every time is YOU. Your personal presentation skills will always have an impact on those presentations in which you participate. As you read this chapter, keep in mind the potential impact of you as a technique.

Objectives

By the end of chapter 8, you will:

- know some ways to combat oral presentation anxiety,
- know methods for improving your oral presentation at various points in the process,
- describe the ARCS Motivation Model and motivational strategies to integrate into an oral presentation,
- understand the importance of active listening,
- know how media can be used to enhance oral presentations, and
- understand the effects of different nonverbal communication cues.

Speaking in Public

Did you know that the greatest fear of Americans is public speaking? Some rate it as more terrifying even than death, sickness, and flying in airplanes. Therefore, you can anticipate some nervousness before you have to speak; the trick is to keep it under control. If you are feeling panicky, then it will certainly negatively affect your presentation.

If you find you have any or all of the following physical manifestations before speaking in public, it's a sure sign that you are not keeping your anxiety under control:

- shaky knees
- cold, sweaty palms

- quick, shallow breathing
- heart palpitations
- dizziness or light-headedness
- feelings of panic
- constant checking for the nearest exit

If any of these characteristics are in your repertoire, you will need to overcome your anxiety. Here are three sure-fire ways to do it: (1) practice, (2) more practice, (3) even more practice! Remember, ERROR is a big part of TERROR and you want to eliminate both from you presentation. Practice will help accomplish this.

Your confidence and ease in oral presentations will grow if you thoroughly prepare, know your content, and build a sold background of experience in creating and implementing oral presentations. While rehearsal is the most effective way to reduce oral presentation anxiety, here are some other helpful tips for preparing and delivering oral presentations that will help you overcome your speaking anxiety.

Preparing Your Presentation

1. Use note cards. Put only an outline of your presentation on the cards. This means you must know your subject matter well enough that only a few words will trigger your knowledge. Avoid writing your speech out, word-for-word on paper. This will likely make you more nervous, as you could possibly lose your place, causing greater anxiety and a less effective presentation.

—Presentation Tip—

If you feel you must write out every word of your presentation, use your finger as a placeholder as you present so that you can look up from the paper from time to time while keeping your place.

---

2. Go through your complete presentation in front of an audience at least three times. Grab your spouse, your roommate, your children, your neighbor, your dog ... anyone who will listen and give you constructive feedback.

3. Time yourself. As you practice, evaluate, and revise your presentation, you will find your efficiency will improve and you can deliver that presentation in exactly the right amount of time. Then prepare a little more. It's useful to have some *extra* information to "pull out of your hat," if needed. It's also useful to identify the in-

formation you can eliminate, in case your presentation is cut short due to time limitations.

4. Go through your complete revised presentation at least two more times. The more you practice, the better you will internalize what you want to say and the more confident you will feel.

Just Before You Present

1. Arrive early. This way you can check out the room, the equipment, the acoustics, etc. to be sure everything is the way you want it. If it isn't, you'll have time to make changes or adjust to the way it is.
2. Mingle with your audience. Meet some of the "early birds" and get to know something about them. This will help relax you (and them) and increase their positive feelings about you. You may also have opportunities to use their names and information about them during your presentation. This conveys friendliness and an attitude that you value your audience.
3. Review your notes. It is helpful to go over your presentation one last time, just before you give it. This way it will be fresh in your mind.
4. Try any or all of the following activities just before your presentation to help you relax: yawn, take a deep breath, touch the floor, shrug your shoulders, shake your body.

During Your Presentation

When we talked about your audience in chapter 3, we described those who would receive your presentation. But there is another important audience for your presentation—YOU! Your audience will give you back verbal and nonverbal feedback throughout your presentation. Will you be able to pick up on their messages? We'll get back to this topic later in the chapter.

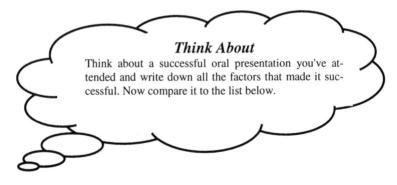

Think About

Think about a successful oral presentation you've attended and write down all the factors that made it successful. Now compare it to the list below.

We have developed a simple mnemonic that guarantees a successful presentation. Try applying it the next time you give an oral presentation.

How Do You Spell S-U-C-C-E-S-S?

There are a number of presentation traits to ensure that your presentation is a SUCCESS:

Strong Presence. A manner that projects confidence and poise conveys the sense that you are enjoying your presentation.

Use of Effective Hook and Persuasive Sinker. A smooth and powerful opening grabs the attention of your audience. A persuasive close that summarizes key points leaves your audience wanting more.

Credibility. Knowing your subject matter, citing your sources, and demonstrating effective presentation skills are some ways to ensure that your audience perceives you as a credible presenter of information.

Contact. Making eye contact with everyone in the audience or, in the case of a large audience, slowly sweeping the room with your eyes as you speak gives members of your audience the impression that you are speaking directly to them.

Enthusiasm. Enthusiasm is contagious; facial expressions and moderate gestures can enhance and reinforce your words. Some sweeping gestures can be appropriate with large audiences. E could also stand for empathy. A natural manner, pleasant tone of voice, and easy-going pace provide a comfortable atmosphere for your audience.

Satisfactory Appearance. Remember, you only have one opportunity to make a first impression. Appropriate dress can contribute to the audience's perception of your credibility and competence. Certain colors of dress also convey a message; red and black convey power and confidence for women, navy blue and dark gray communicate authority and credibility for men. Moderation is the key to appearance; judicious use of makeup, avoidance of flashy jewelry and outlandish clothing, and eliminating distracting mannerisms will help keep your audience's attention where you want it.

Sincerity. Conveying a genuineness and honest commitment to your topic will contribute to a positive relationship between presenter and audience.

Think About

Think about a successful oral presentation you've attended and write down all the factors that made it successful. Now compare it to the list above.

Voice as Technique

Your voice may serve as a technique for gaining the attention and confidence of your audience. There are four characteristics that you need to
consider: rate, volume, pitch, and articulation.[1]

Rate

The rate or speed at which you speak can convey subtle messages to
your audience. Speaking too fast projects nervousness; speaking too
slowly may convey to your audience that you are unsure of your material. Controlling the pace of your presentation by speaking in a deliberate manner with appropriate intonations and occasional pauses that
allow your audience to think about what you're saying is critical for
effective presentations.

Volume

Volume refers to the loudness of your voice. You will want to vary
your volume to avoid sounding monotone—a speaking trait most audiences find a major cause of boredom. Volume is an important factor in
voice projection. Try aiming your voice at a specific target with adequate volume to effectively project your voice. Adequate volume also
will help convey a sense of confidence to your audience.

Pitch

An excessively high- or low-pitched voice can be distracting to your message and quite irritating to your audience. A well-modulated voice will allow your audience to focus on what you are saying rather than how you are saying it and will also help with voice projection. Occasionally varying the pitch adds interest to an oral presentation.

Articulation

How well you pronounce your words will have a direct bearing on how well your message is received. Be clear and concise, pronounce every syllable, and don't chop off words or drop your voice at the end of a word.

Try this for fun. Say one or more of the following sentences with precise articulation:

- The king was singing while shopping and swinging.
  (Did you remember to pronounce every ending g?)
- The dazzling duke dragged the dizzy dragon down into the deep, dark, dank, dreary dungeon.
- Lazy lizards sizzle in a drizzle; prize lizards are wizards with scissors and puzzles.
- She sells short shirts and shells in the shop near the shore.
  (Be sure to control each "s" so that you pronounce it rather than whistle it.)

Somebody's boring me...I think it's me.

Dylan Thomas

Motivators as Technique

No matter what type or format of presentation you are preparing, the use of motivational techniques can add to its overall effectiveness. For presentations in which the broad purpose is to inspire, instruct, or influence the audience, you will want to incorporate motivational strategies and sprinkle them throughout. Motivational strategies may play a somewhat less important role if the purpose of the presentation is simply to inform as in presenting a new policy, procedure, budget, etc.; however, you will still need to incorporate *some* motivational strategies in order to sustain attention and prevent boredom. For example, high-lighting important text, leaving lots of white space, and adding colorful graphics are simple attention devices you can use as motivational strategies for a written presentation such as a brochure or newsletter; changing the pace, raising or lowering the volume of your voice, and adding an activity to get the audience involved can increase interest in an oral presentation.

Motivators help *spice up* your presentation. While they are impor-tant for all presentation techniques (e.g., oral, written, multimedia), we discuss them in this chapter as a way to help take a good oral presenta-tion and make it great. To do this, we describe a simple, but powerful motivation model, the ARCS Model of Motivational Design, developed by Professor John Keller of Florida State University.[2]

The ARCS Model

The ARCS Model is based on a number of motivation theories, most notably expectancy-value theory (E-V theory), a theory most com-monly associated with the research of Victor Vroom in the 1960s.[3] E-V theory states that for a person to be motivated, two factors must be in place—*value* and *expectancy for success.* Applied to presentations, these factors can be defined as how much the audience values the pres-entation and whether audience members believe they can understand or learn from the presentation. Although the ARCS Model was designed for application to instructing presentations, we find it can be applied to other types as well. We believe that the thoughtful incorporation of appropriate motivational strategies guarantees a dynamite presentation!

The ARCS Model identifies four essential strategy components that can be incorporated into presentations to increase your audience's motivation. They are:

[A]ttention strategies for arousing and sustaining your audience's inter-est and curiosity.

[R]elevance strategies that link your content to your audience's needs, interests, and motives.

[C]onfidence strategies that help your audience develop positive expec-tations about your presentation.

[S]atisfaction strategies that provide extrinsic and intrinsic reinforce-ment to your audience.

Relating these four components to E-V theory, attention and rele-vance strategies help to create *value* while confidence and satisfaction strategies help create a positive *expectancy for success.* Let's break down the ARCS Model into each of its components, identifying spe-cific tactics that you may want to use in your presentations.

Think About

Before reading the list of tactics below, think about a recent effective presentation when you were in the audience. Think about who presented, what information was presented, and in what format. Try to recapture the total presentation in your mind. Now read the list of motivation tactics, and think about which ones were used in this presentation and how they contributed to its overall success.

Attention

The ARCS Model specifies that is not only important to gain your audience's attention *at the beginning* of a presentation but it is essential to sustain their attention *throughout* your presentation. These attention-grabbers might provide just the right *hook* for your presentation.

Introduce incongruity or conflict. You might begin a presentation by playing devil's advocate by making a startling statement that will cause conflict in the audience's mind. Let's say you are speaking before a concerned group of parents considering guidelines for healthy behavior. You might begin your presentation with the following statement: "Cigarette smoking is not harmful to your health." This should stimulate a lively discussion. Now that you have your audience's attention, you can follow up with an admission that we all know this is not true, given the research now available, and proceed to discuss your topic.

Incorporate humor. Injecting a humorous story, cartoon or one liner that is relevant to your content can be effective not only for gaining the attention of your audience but also for creating a friendly atmosphere for your presentation. But be careful; make sure that you are comfortable with humor and that your use of humor is understandable and will not be construed as offensive by some or all of your audience.

For example, avoid ethnic or culturally sensitive humor that might be considered offensive by members of your audience.

Ask questions. Inserting questions at various points in your presentation helps to engage your audience. Questions can be *rhetorical* (something for them to think about as you proceed through your presentation) or *actual* (something you want them to respond to at that moment). Make sure, however, that if it's an actual question, you provide enough *wait time*, a concept described by researcher Mary Budd Rowe.[4] Believe it or not, most presenters wait less than a second before jumping in to answer their own question; perhaps they feel uncomfortable with the silence. If you rush to answer without giving at least a few seconds for your audience to contemplate your question and process an answer, this technique can become ineffective. Provide at least three to five seconds for a response to your questions. You may find that you have more responses and better, more thoughtful responses.

Provide variety. Here is your opportunity to incorporate a range of techniques and media to meet your audience's varying needs. The use of different types of information (e.g., charts, flowcharts), audio-visuals (e.g., videos, overhead transparencies), and varying the pacing/timing of your presentation will help sustain your audience's attention and interest.

Provide opportunities for participation. When your audience is involved and participating, it is engaged. Some methods for increasing audience participation are by including:

- a question and answer period,
- small group discussions,
- a brief brainstorming or role playing activity,
- a quick exercise (e.g., filling out a survey, completing a puzzle), or
- just asking the audience to think about something specific as they listen to your presentation (like the "Think About" activities in this book).

Relevance

While you may think your presentation is the best thing since sliced bread, your audience may have a harder time understanding the WIFT. Whether your presentation is in the form of a written report or an oral presentation, there are a number of techniques you can use to increase its relevance for your audience. Here are a few specific suggestions:

Share experiences. Personal anecdotes that illustrate specific key points in your presentation help to make it memorable and more meaningful to your audience. They may be from your own experience, from the audience members themselves, or presented by outsiders, such as in a video testimonial.

Match your audience's needs. In chapter 2, we discussed the importance of understanding your audience's incoming needs. Once you know what's important to your audience members, you can plan a presentation that is in harmony with their goals, interests, preferences, or motives. For example, some people prefer visual information while others prefer a written format. Therefore, the use of videos or computer-based presentation software supplemented with text-based handouts would speak to these needs. Some people are more holistic; they like to get the big picture first. Others prefer to start with the details leading up to the big picture. Providing an agenda or overview at the beginning and a summary or recap at the end will address these varying needs.

Remember in chapter 3 when we discussed achievement motivation and the three needs? We explained that people are motivated in different ways: some by power, others by affiliation, others by achievement, or some combination. Varying activities that allow your audience to participate and/or interact are important techniques for satisfying these different needs.

Confidence

Your audience members may experience some apprehension about your presentation, either because your content is new or unfamiliar to them or they don't know what to expect. Here are some techniques that will help boost confidence. This can have a profound effect on their perceptions of their ability to understand your presentation (this is especially true for presentations that include a great deal of technical and/or abstract information).

Clarify expectations. Let your audience know what it can expect from your presentation at the very beginning. One way of accomplishing this is to set an agenda. Then, review the agenda from time to time during your presentation. Also let them know what you expect from them, including what they are expected to do during the presentation or know at the end.

> *To listen well is as powerful a means of communication and influence as to talk well.*
>
> John Marshall, first Chief Justice of the U.S. Supreme Court

Actively listen. You've probably heard the saying "Good listening is an important part of effective speaking." As an active listening presenter, you need to focus on what your audience communicates to you, not only through words but also by voice tone and volume as well as through body language. When an audience member is asking a question, concentrate, maintain eye contact, don't interrupt, and don't let other things distract you. If you're not sure you have heard things correctly, ask for clarification. Sometimes you'll need to probe for additional information, just to be sure you understand the full intent of the question.

Give feedback. Giving good feedback is also an important part of being an active listening presenter. One common type of feedback is giving answers to questions asked by your audience. But what happens if you don't know the answer to a question? Remember, no one can be expected to know everything about any topic. While it isn't your responsibility to know all the answers, it is your responsibility to get the answers. Perhaps someone in the audience can help. If not, you can tell the questioner you will find out the answer to his or her question and communicate it at a later time (to an individual or the entire audience), in person, via email, or another communication medium.

Satisfaction

Generally speaking, an audience will leave satisfied if your presentation was consistent with their expectations and perceived as rewarding. Here are a few suggestions.

Encourage intrinsic satisfaction. Intrinsic satisfiers are those whose value comes from within the audience members themselves. For example, a person who attends your informing oral presentation simply because they are interested in the topic and want to learn more about it (not because it is a requirement of their job) is said to be *intrinsically motivated.* Perhaps, there is something you can add to your presentation for those audience members who find your presentation intrinsically satisfying, such as providing a handout with additional readings and Internet sites where they can find out more about the topic of interest.

Provide extrinsic rewards. These can be very effective when delivering presentations within your own workplace. Imagine how good your audience would feel if, on the way out of your presentation, you handed each one an unexpected reward (e.g., a certificate of accomplishment). Simple spoken praise for attending your presentation can also be an effective extrinsic motivator. Providing a variety of expected *perks* that an audience perceives they will receive as a result of your presentation, either for accepting what it is you are selling or simply for attending, can also be enormously satisfying. These can range from money to special privileges. Both intrinsic and extrinsic motivators are useful for increasing satisfaction, but intrinsic motivators will have a more long-term effect.

This section has described motivational strategies to consider when creating an oral presentation. As you make decisions about which strategies to use, remember that more is not always better. Too many strategies can make an audience anxious, while too few can result in boredom. We recommend the "Goldilocks approach"—decide which and how many strategies are *just right* for your audience.

Think About

Now that you know a variety of motivational presentation strategies, think about how they might also be applied to written presentations and, as you read chapter 9, how they can be applied to the design or multimedia presentations.

Media Matters

Media are methods of communication used to transmit a message from a sender to a receiver. Media can stand on their own or supplement and enhance other types of presentations. Videotapes, audiotapes, models, flipcharts, overhead transparencies (and combinations of these), as well as computer technology, are types of media commonly used in presentations.

Don't lose sight of the rules for visual media regarding lettering, color, and static vs. moving images that we described in chapter 5 when determining how to use media in your presentation.

Why Use Media?

There are many reasons to incorporate media into a presentation. First, media can store and deliver information efficiently. They can also help make abstract or complicated information simpler and more concrete than with simply verbal or written explanation. Media communicate and reinforce messages in forms that appeal to different cognitive styles. Finally, media are motivational; they add variety to oral presentations.

There are some questions to be answered when selecting a medium for use in an oral presentation:

- How much will I use the medium in my presentation?
- Is it cost-effective?
- Is the technology of sufficient quality to be effective?
- Are the hardware and/or software accessible and easy to get?
- Does the medium fit the purpose of my presentation?
- Does the presentation environment allow the effective use of this medium? (e.g., Are the acoustics good? Can the room be darkened, if necessary?)
- Does the size of the audience dictate one medium over another?

- Are there characteristics of my audience that dictate one medium over another? (e.g., Senior citizens may benefit from projected slides that enlarge visuals or text used with an oral presentation; videos may help to maintain the attention of an audience of children.)
- Does the nature of my content dictate one medium over another?

Printed handouts may be used for quite some time after the presentation is over; they may contain some details about your content, such as some references to materials used to prepare the presentation. Overhead transparencies, slides, and other still images supplement your spoken message; they do not replace it.

Computer-based multimedia technology is quickly becoming the most common medium used in presentations. It is an incredibly flexible medium—interactive, multiple media, and multiple applications. We discuss multimedia presentations in detail in chapter 9.

You as Medium

You are an important medium in your oral presentation. Let your personality shine through!

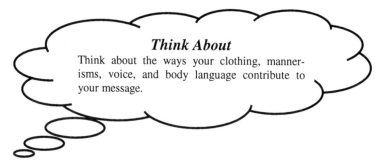

Think About

Think about the ways your clothing, mannerisms, voice, and body language contribute to your message.

Non-Verbal Communication: Why Is It Important?

Perhaps there have been times when what you thought someone was communicating through non-verbal communication was really something very different. It becomes very confusing when, for example, you interpret one's glazed over look to mean "You are boring me!" when it could be that he or she is just over-tired from lack of sleep. The message is unrelated to your presentation, but not knowing the other person's situation, you misinterpret its meaning. On the other hand, you as presenter may be guilty of conveying negative messages through nonverbal cues from time to time, as well. By learning about non-verbal communication, you will become more aware of the cues we read and give and become less likely to convey the wrong meaning to others.

Forms of Non-Verbal Communication

Have you ever thought about the types of nonverbal cues you give? Did you know that body language (your posture, gestures, facial expressions) can communicate more to your audience than your voice and words combined? Body language can convey some powerful, visual cues (both positive and negative) to your audience, adding more, or sometimes different, meaning to your words. For example, a slouching posture can project uncertainty and insecurity, even when your words indicate expertise on your topic.

Spatial cues, the distances we assume when communicating with others, convey messages. In American culture, standing too close to someone as you speak can create an uncomfortable situation. Less than eighteen inches might be considered an intimate distance while most public presentations require a distance of twelve feet or more.[5] However, occasionally stepping outside the podium area and toward your audience can make your audience feel they are having a more intimate experience. Sometimes you can make a point by standing right next to an individual audience member and engaging (without embarrassing) him or her in some way. Some content may require a more intimate approach.

Top presenters are always aware of body language and only convey what they really want to, using it to their advantage rather than letting it detract from their message. For example, making an "O" (for okay) with your thumb and forefinger is a physical sign that translates to a word or phrase. Clapping and smiling at an audience member's response to a question while saying "Great answer!" reinforces your words and reveals your feelings. Dressing in a business suit, appropriate hairstyle, etc. communicate a professional manner and serious approach to your topic. One must keep in mind, however, that other cultures may interpret any or all of these nonverbal communications as a negative, sometimes even offensive, message. Being aware of cultural differences in body language and nonverbal communication can prevent some potentially embarrassing or disastrous results.

The importance of eye contact as a nonverbal way of communicating cannot be overemphasized. While it is not difficult to make eye contact with a small audience, when the audience is greater than fifty, it becomes more challenging to make everyone in the room feel you are speaking just to them. Try this next time: think of the room as a giant map of the United States, identifying the north, east, south, and west (as well as northeast, southeast, central, northwest, and southwest) locations. Then, think of your presentation as a cross-country trip you are taking with your eyes, slowly make eye contact with each location taking a circular route and then randomly moving from location to location (e.g., traveling from the northeast to the southwest). Practice it and you will find it eventually becomes a natural part of your speaking repertoire.

Some people naturally "speak" with their hands; often these movements reinforce their words. Sometimes, however, hand movements can distract your audience. There are some simple rules for controlling hand gestures. When speaking to a small audience (less than fifty people), think of your body as a rectangle. Then, don't let your hands go outside the rectangle. If you are speaking to a larger audience, make occasionally sweeping gestures to communicate inclusiveness. This is a way of bringing your whole audience into your presentation.

At this point we need to interject a note of caution. In some cultures some of these gestures are interpreted differently. Make sure that if you are speaking to a multicultural or non-American audience, you understand enough about their culture to avoid any offensive or inappropriate body language.

There are a number of common personal habits of presenters that can become distractions for an audience. For example, rattling coins or keys in your pocket, frequently injecting superfluous words or phrases like "uh," "ah," "you know," and "I mean," ring twisting, clearing your throat, ear tugging, beard stroking, finger drumming, lip biting, knuckle cracking, foot tapping, bridge of the glasses pushing, and brushing or tossing hair back from your face are all annoying (albeit unconscious) habits that interfere with the effective transmission of information. They are the human equivalent of radio static, a skip in a CD, and a fluttering video screen. Unfortunately, you cannot wear a sign around your neck that says, "I am experiencing technical difficulties. Please stand by." Instead, you'll need to make a concerted conscious effort to stop them as they can have a negative impact on the effectiveness of your oral presentation.

After Your Presentation

While you may feel some relief after completing your presentation, you are still not done. This is a good time to reflect on your presentation, assessing what went really well and why and what didn't go well and why. Hopefully, you also conducted some type of evaluation that provides feedback from your audience. (Chapter 10 is devoted to describing alternative ways of evaluating your presentation.) Both self-assessment and audience evaluations will provide you with valuable information for improving your presentation the next time.

We end with a sad but true story of a less than successful presentation that one author attended during a national, professional conference. The presenters were two noted researchers so it was a popular session at the conference. The presenters planned an oral presentation supplemented by overhead transparencies. The room was large and the chairs close together so the audience was packed in there pretty tightly (in other words, there was no escape!). There was an overhead projector placed smack dab in the middle of the audience and this author happened to be sitting directly behind it.

As the presenters began their presentation, one walked to the extreme right front corner of the room while the other walked to the extreme left corner of the room. One would say a few sentences, then the other, then back to the first, and so on. It was like watching a tennis match! It was like they were having a casual (unrehearsed) conversation on which 150 people were eavesdropping. This went on for about fifteen minutes. Then it got worse!

One of the presenters, with a folder of overhead transparencies under his arm, made his way to the projector with the intention of using the transparencies to supplement his oral presentation. As he approached the projector and placed one transparency on the projector, he bumped into someone (remember, it was crowded and the projector was placed in the center of the audience) and the rest of his transparencies fell to the floor. As he bent down to pick them up, his elbow hit the top of the projector and the projection mechanism rotated upward toward the ceiling rather then focusing forward on the screen. Now the entire audience was looking up at the ceiling, trying to read the transparency. At this point, the person sitting next to the author slipped her a note that said, "It's a good thing these guys don't have guns!" What should have been an outstanding presentation turned into a Laurel & Hardy imitation. It was apparent that the presenters had not practiced nor adequately prepared their presentation. To say their audience left dissatisfied is an understatement!

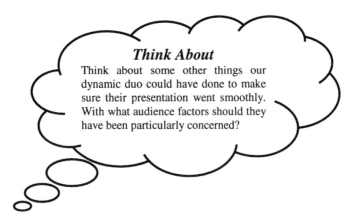

Think About

Think about some other things our dynamic duo could have done to make sure their presentation went smoothly. With what audience factors should they have been particularly concerned?

Let's Hear It! ◄))

When Sullivan County (NY) decided to change its form of government from a Board of Supervisors to an elected County Legislature, an annual dinner/fundraising event was initiated to introduce the Democratic legislative candidates to both the party officials and the public at large. At this event, whoever is running for office in the county is highlighted, given a platform, and introduced. Any money that comes to a Democratic candidate's campaign comes from this fundraiser unless the candidate decides to hold private fundraisers. "This was a new form of government; the county had previously had a Board of Supervisors. So to go into a charter form of government and having legislators coming after almost 200 years of supervisors was a very, very big deal in the county," says Leni Binder, one of nine Democratic candidates in that historic race. "The press was rabid; they followed us everywhere," Leni declares. There were nineteen candidates (for nine legislative slots with one district having a three-way race).

The audience consisted of approximately 250 people, including every Democratic delegate in the county, spouses, people involved in government, businesspeople, anyone involved in politics, and lots and lots of press. The event was held in a hotel in the county, just a few short weeks before the election.

Each of the nine Democratic candidates was allotted approximately three minutes to introduce themselves, present their platform, and make a statement. The purpose of the presentation was three-fold. First it was an influencing presentation. As Leni explained, "I pretty much assumed everybody there would vote for me because they were Democrats but I had to encourage them in these three minutes to get their friends to go out and campaign for me, not just vote for me. I was also looking for endorsements from the press. So there was a lot riding on it." It was an informing presentation because background information about each candidate was provided in the form of brochures and press releases. It also needed to be an inspiring presentation to motivate people to campaign for their candidate over the Republican opponent. The problem was: how do you accomplish all of that in just *three* minutes???

"I was considered a real underdog. I had never run for office before. My opponent was an elected coroner and a retired policeman. He was a little league coach and an umpire so he was well known and he had a great campaign theme. His last name was Green so the color green became an integral part of his campaign—his brochures were green, his bumper stickers were green, his buttons were green. All you had to do was look at it and you had this whole visual effect." Leni said.

"The fact that I, as a redhead, had always worn the color green was an issue for me," Leni went on. "So I stopped wearing the color green and people began to comment on it. I stuck to wearing gold tones and I made my signs black and gold. I stayed as far away from green as possible. This gave me an idea for my three-minute presentation. I decided that in three minutes I couldn't tell them anything more about me personally that they didn't already know from my brochure and press bios. Since people had noticed I had stopped wearing green, I decided to go for a cute approach and add some humor regarding the color green. I had written out a very brief statement, saying who I was, that I was a native of the county, that I was very happy for this opportunity, that I was campaigning very hard, that we had all had to make sacrifices, and that my biggest sacrifice was having to give up my favorite color— green! And that's all I was going to say and sit down. I had rehearsed it and it had gone over well."

The use of humor can create a friendly, relaxed tone for your presentation. It can also provide a memorable moment for your audience, especially when you have a very limited amount of time to make a significant impression. So, Leni's approach seemed like it would be a great success.

Well, it was memorable but not in the way Leni wanted. "I didn't really know where the hotel was; I had been there once before but I had never driven the route. It was really out in the boondocks with no major road to it so you're literally going through wheat fields and cornfields, which were all higher than the car. Thus, we got lost and I was afraid we'd be late. By the time I arrived, I was a nervous wreck."

Leni probably should have driven to the hotel at least once before the day of the event to be sure she knew the way. She also should have checked out the room and the equipment. Here's what happened next. "I arrived late and anxious and the person who got up to speak before me was about 6'3" (I'm 5'3")," Leni recounted. "Nobody moved the microphone for me. I got up there nervous; I couldn't reach the microphone and I couldn't pull it down. Static started; I began to panic and I started mumbling. I read my whole speech in just one and a half minutes and the only thing the audience heard was the last word—GREEN!"

Being familiar with technical equipment and knowing how to adjust, fix, or do without it is an important skill for presenters. Murphy's Law states "What can go wrong will go wrong," and this is certainly true when it comes to the use of technology in presentations. Moreover, this wasn't the first time Leni had had problems with microphones. "As I thought about this experience, I remembered a similar experience in high school when, as an honor student, I was to give a speech at graduation. I had problems with the microphone; I repeated my speech three times continually tapping the microphone. Now that I think about it, no one had ever taught me to use a microphone since then. "

While nothing could reverse what happened that memorable night in October, Leni learned an important lesson. "Interestingly enough," she related, "after that fiasco I sat with someone who worked for a radio station and told him, 'You've *got* to teach me to use a microphone!' And he did. I've since learned to use hand-held ones and I have never had problems since then. So I think the key here is that if you learn from this and grow with it it's fine. If you let it take over your life, you will never be able to speak in public. You will expect yourself to fail, and you will. There will always be mechanical failures and if you don't deal with them, you'll never have a command of the people you're speaking to, you won't trust yourself to do it." This is great advice for any oral presenter. And, by the way, there *is* a happy ending to this story. Despite the rocky start, Leni won the election and is now serving her second term as majority leader of the Sullivan County Legislature!

Generating Ideas at DD Inc.

Alexis Pollanis, Director of Human Resources at DD Inc., suggests that the team brainstorm a "Presenter's Checklist" that they can all use as a "dos and don'ts" reference for designing and giving effective oral presentations. Each of the team members contributes to the list.

Effective Oral Presentations

Dos
___ Prepare note cards.
___ Rehearse your presentation.
___ Establish rapport.
___ Be enthusiastic.
___ Be an active listener.
___ Make eye contact.

Don'ts
___ Wear flashy jewelry.
___ Use fillers like "um" and "you know."
___ Pace back and forth.
___ Speak in a monotone.
___ Misinterpret audience body language.
___ Read your material.

Alexis decides to incorporate their ideas into a job aid for members of the team to use when preparing their next oral presentation.

Learning Check

1. Name some methods for relieving oral presentation anxiety.

2. What are the ten traits for ensuring presentation SUCCESS?

3. What are four characteristics of your voice to consider when delivering an oral presentation?

4. What is the purpose of the ARCS Model?

5. What theory provides the foundation for the ARCS Model?

6. What are the four components of the ARCS Model?

7. What ARCS component does each of the following motivational strategies address:

    a. Incorporate humor.
    b. Provide extrinsic rewards.
    c. Clarify expectations.
    d. Ask a question.
    e. Match audience needs.
    f. Actively listen.
    g. Share experiences.

8. What can media contribute to a presentation?

9. What are some helpful and some distracting body language communicators?

10. What is a good practice following each presentation?

Do & Discuss

Suppose that you are the marketing director for an environmental organization that is fighting the building of a new waste management facility in your audience's area. You have been given an opportunity to present at a county meeting on behalf of your organization. Your audience, however, has been promised a reduction in taxes if they vote to have the facility in their area. Ask yourself:

• What motivational techniques might you use to increase the relevance of the issue to your audience so that they see the potential dangers? We know you are probably not an expert in this area so just be creative!

Make a list of all the motivators described in this chapter. Then:

• As you observe an oral presentation (e.g., a class, a guest speaker), check off all the motivators you observe in that one session.

- What motivators seem to be used most often? least often? most effectively?

Videotape yourself doing a brief oral presentation. Watch the tape, identifying your presentation strengths and pinpointing areas for improvement. Experiment with different voice rates, volumes, and pitches. Then re-tape your presentation and look for improvement.

The team at DD Inc. made a good start on a presenter's dos & don'ts list but their list is incomplete. It's time for you to reflect on what you have learned in this chapter and other chapters and add your ideas to their list. Now, take your list and evaluate someone else's presentation.

Observe an oral presentation either live or on TV. Use your dos & don'ts list to evaluate the presentation. Add any new dos and don'ts that you recognize in the presentation.

Coming Up...

We now move on to the technique that combines several media into one presentation—multimedia presentations. Chapter 9 looks at stand-alone multimedia (e.g., kiosks, CD-ROMs), multimedia used in conjunction with oral presentations (e.g., computer-based presentation software such as PowerPoint), and Web-based multimedia presentations.

Notes

1. Hank Staley, *Tongue & Quill: Your Practical (and Humorous) Guide to Better Communication* (Washington, D.C.: Pergamon-Brassey's International Defense Publishers, Inc., 1990), 95-98.
2. John M. Keller, "Strategies for Stimulating the Motivation to Learn," *Performance & Instruction* 26, no. 8 (October 1987): 1-7.
3. Victor Vroom, *Work and Motivation* (New York: Wiley, 1964).

4. Mary Budd Rowe, "Wait Time: Slowing Down May Be a Way of Speeding Up!" *Journal of Teacher Education* 37, no.1 (January-February1986): 43-50.

5. Richard L. Weaver II, *Understanding Interpersonal Communication*, 4th ed. (Glenview, IL: Scott, Foresman and Company, 1987), 176-179.

Chapter 9

T Is for Technique:
Multimedia Presentations

PACT Model©

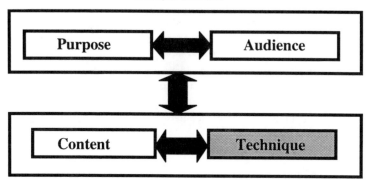

Throughout the previous chapters, we have discussed the importance of defining a clear overall purpose, conducting a thorough audience analysis to genuinely understand their specific needs, and creating a clear-cut structure for content presentation. In this chapter, multimedia is presented as a powerful technique for both enhancing presentations you deliver in person and for creating stand-alone presentations. The purpose of this chapter is to introduce you to a number of multimedia concepts and issues as they relate to information presentation. We will use actual examples from multimedia work conducted by Creative Media Solutions, a firm owned by one of the authors, to help illustrate these concepts. While this chapter can serve as a brief introduction to multimedia, readers are encouraged to explore the many available texts dedicated to this topic for more comprehensive coverage.

Objectives

By the end of chapter 9, you should be able to:

- define multimedia and identify the presentation uses of it,
- identify important upfront considerations when planning multimedia presentations including the decision to create a prototype,
- describe additional content dimensions for multimedia,
- describe several design documents and how they are used,
- understand the importance of project management and periodic reality checks,
- identify tasks related to videos for multimedia,
- explain the importance of establishing validation criteria for testing your interactive presentation, and
- understand the difference between alpha and beta testing.

New technologies provide extraordinary, almost supernatural, powers to those who master them.

Ben Shneiderman, p. 2

What Is Multimedia?

Multimedia is a term that has been loosely defined for years but actually takes on different meanings depending on the situation. Basically, multimedia brings together multiple types of media, which can include text, audio, video, graphics, photos, and animations. In its simplest form, interactivity is not required; in fact, it could be a combination of the elements mentioned above compiled into a slide show or video. However, multimedia can include a wide array of platforms and uses. Virtually all of today's multimedia presentations are given in some digital form with the most effective uses of multimedia combining interactive components. In the next section, we will examine several uses of multimedia.

Uses of Multimedia

Corporate training, sales and marketing, interactive education, interactive games, and presentations and communications are the most common uses of multimedia. Any of these can include a variety of media from video, CD-ROM, DVD, and the Web.

This text will focus on presentations and communications, although aspects of the others can be involved. Multimedia presentations might be *automated*, *presenter-facilitated*, or *user-facilitated*. Automated multimedia presentations can be seen in a variety of contexts including trade shows, kiosks placed in airports or lobbies of organizations, and with information distributed in any digital format. This type of multimedia presentation follows a *linear format* and is programmed to begin at specific times or to loop and re-play itself. It is considered multimedia because it uses a variety of media in its presentation. It could be as simple as a videotape (an analog medium) that incorporates these elements.

When used in conjunction with presenter-facilitated oral presentations, multimedia takes the role of *supporting or reinforcing* what the live presenter is saying. Most commonly, it is incorporated through presentation software such as MS PowerPoint. The presenter uses a combination of text, graphics, audio, video, hypertext links and possibly hyperlinks to other programs, and the Web for supporting information to achieve his or her goals. The presenter controls the pacing of the elements and the sequencing of the content. Thus, *the presenter plays the central role in this use of multimedia.*

From conference rooms to large auditoriums, presenter-facilitated multimedia are most common. They can be linear or interactive; that is, they can follow a prescribed path through the presentation or can allow for interactive components. For example, the presenter might construct his presentation using a menu that adds value by allowing flexibility based on audience response. In one presentation, one of the co-authors created a menu at the beginning of her PowerPoint presentation with links to six topics that she hoped to cover. Since a linear progression was not required, she was able to discern from her audience where the greatest interest was and proceed from there.

The audience of a multimedia presentation can vary from a single person to "the world." (Members of a multimedia audience are often referred to as *users*.) User-facilitated multimedia presentations *focus on giving the user control and generally incorporate varying degrees of interactivity.* At the low end the user can, at a minimum, control the pacing and selection of content. As the degree of interactivity increases, the user can input information and change the content based on individual needs. The user's input then becomes a part of the end product. At the most sophisticated levels, the multimedia system tracks user choices and learns user preferences to respond more accurately to user needs. Sophisticated multimedia systems often include large information databases. The three types of multimedia presentations described above, their distinguishing features, and major uses are represented in figure 9.1.

MULTIMEDIA	DISTINGUISHING FEATURES	MAJOR USES
Automated	Stand-alone, no interactivity (except to start or stop), linear and passive, no speaker support	Kiosks, trade shows, accessed directly from home through Web, or sent via mail (Examples: CD-ROM, DVD, videos)
Presenter-facilitated	Support role, presenter controls presentation, can be linear or interactive	Conference rooms with audience, classrooms, auditoriums, etc.
User-facilitated	User-centered, one-on-one, interactive	Same uses as automated but can include large multimedia databases

Figure 9.1. Types of Multimedia Presentations

Important Upfront Considerations

Creativity and expertise in your designated area is critical to the success of any project. Wouldn't it be great to have unlimited resources to fully unleash your creative ideas? The reality is, however, that generally we must work within certain parameters. Budgetary constraints, available resources, and time are some of them. If your project involves designing a basic multimedia presentation including graphics, text, and simple animations, you may be able to accomplish everything yourself, especially if you are proficient with presentation software like PowerPoint. Let's assume, however, that you must design a sophisticated interactive presentation that may become a CD-ROM, DVD, or Web site. You will most likely require the services of others.

Remember, in chapter 2 when we stated that the other part of *P* in the PACT Approach is Planning? It becomes especially important for such projects as interactive multimedia presentations. Planning includes estimating your production costs, personnel needs, and addressing a number of other upfront considerations.

Planning a Budget

Assuming you are the project manager of your own presentation, you will need to establish a budget for your project. Research and prior experience can provide the basis for estimating your budget. Once you have roughed out a projected budget, ask someone who has done similar projects for feedback. The challenge will then be to adhere to the bottom line that you have established and have had approved.

Scripts, storyboards, and flowcharts are helpful in planning and budgeting an intensive project. A simple flowchart is useful for brainstorming the overall structure of your project at its onset; a detailed flowchart to accompany written documentation can greatly assist a programmer on complex projects. Scripts, flowcharts, and storyboards will be discussed later in this chapter.

Explore and identify existing resources that are available and appropriate. For example, are there graphics that were produced for other projects that can also be incorporated into your presentation? Perhaps, you can excerpt a suitable video clip from a pre-existing video produced by your organization. This is referred to as *repurposing* existing resources and will save on production costs.

One important caveat we would like to make about repurposing existing materials is this: Do *not* use poor copies of existing resources in a new presentation. You will have inferior results. It is like the weakest link in a chain. Always find the original whenever possible, especially where video is concerned. Because it is often difficult to fully establish exact costs upfront for every aspect of your project (especially unforeseen delays or additional expenses), it is wise to include as substantial a contingency fund as possible.

—PRESENTATION TIP—
If at all possible, always include a contingency fund!

Legal Concerns

Often, you will find a perfect graphic, video excerpt, or music selection to accompany your presentation that exactly fits your needs, but it is from an outside source. If you or your organization do not own the rights to the material, the question becomes—can you use it legally? Make sure to acquire written copyright permission from the original source of the material that you wish to include in your presentation. Some resources are available in exchange for payment of royalties or for licensing fees.

If your project is a large one that will be disseminated on a national or international scale, you should by all means have legal counsel in such matters. In fact, many organizations will also demand that all contracts or sub-contracts are cleared through their legal department even for small projects. This is important, for example, if you are subcontracting the writing, graphics design, or other elements of your multimedia presentation to agencies or individuals outside your organization.

If your project is a large one, you may even wish to publish a request for proposals (RFP) and distribute it to possible sources of the services you need. This way you can describe your needs and then decide which source will offer you the best service at the best possible price. What you cannot repurpose or acquire from outside sources with permission will require original production. That brings us to the next upfront consideration: managing a team who will help you create your presentation.

Think About
What are some factors that would influence your decision regarding selection of existing vs. creation of original materials to use in a multimedia presentation?

Managing a Team

You may need to assemble a team with expertise in the required areas. Team members may include graphic artists, technical staff such as programmers and video/audio production crew, writers, instructional designers, researchers, and so on.

Flashback

In chapter 2, we talked about being a presentation project manager. You, as project manager, will be the one that keeps the overall vision of the project intact for the team, helping your team stay focused and directed.

You will have to manage the timeline and budget. A projected timeline for the completion of each task is essential at the start of the project. Noting task dependencies—that is, which tasks can be started only after subordinate tasks are completed—is also important. Timeline delays will obviously result in budget overruns and you will be surprised at how fast time flies when developing multimedia projects! One way of keeping on time and on budget is through excellent communications.

Communicating with team members on a regular basis is critical. It is easy to assume that each player is an expert at what they do and that "butting in" may be resented during the creation process. However, it is just the opposite. Feedback is needed, and leaving your production team to themselves too long may result in a product that differs substantially from your original vision.

Flashback

Remember the ARCS motivational model? ARCS can be applied to interpersonal communications as well as information presentations. So hone your motivational skills in order to use appropriate strategies for dealing with the different individuals on your team. Some will require praise for continued good work; others will require informative feedback to get them back on track if they run into difficulties. Do it at regular intervals so team members will know how they are progressing.

Let team members know your expectations for communicating progress to you from the start. Perhaps it is weekly meetings or emails, or even a more sophisticated system that you could arrange with the help of an application like Microsoft Project or a Web-based project management program if your team members are geographically dispersed. Such programs are excellent for developing timelines and task dependencies. Not only do you need to receive updates on team members' progress, the team as a whole should receive regular overviews from you so that each member (especially those who prefer a *holistic* approach) understands his or her contribution to the whole.

—PRESENTATION TIP—

Make sure that your project team members know your expectations for communicating progress to you from the start!

The Prototype Decision

Another upfront consideration is whether to create a *prototype* or not. A prototype is a sample of your project. It could be one piece or module of the project created to mirror the look and feel of a completed project or it could be a mock-up of the completed project with limited functionality to test the overall concept. The purpose of a prototype is to help in decision-making with regard to the final product before a large expenditure of money is made. Producing a prototype does cost more upfront but could result in cost savings down the line if problems are identified in the prototype and corrected.

In one project undertaken by the authors, the development of a prototype proved extremely useful. We had designed a multimedia information system for educators to help them generate ideas for teaching research skills to children in elementary school. We developed an initial prototype and had representatives from the target audience review it. Having members of the target audience review the first iteration prototype saved much time and many dollars. The results provided a great deal of direction for both content and development issues including the intuitiveness of the prototype, the clarity of search categories, the need to reduce the number of search variables, and so on.

Reality Checks

Finally, it is important that you conduct regular reality checks. Ask yourself: where *are* we and where *should* we be with regard to the timeline and budget? React to challenges and correct problems as they occur rather than waiting until problems get out of hand, your budget whirls out of control, and possibly even your professional reputation is damaged. Consider using tools like PERT or GANTT charts to create timelines for tasks and deliverables.

Additional Purpose and Audience Considerations

With multimedia, other considerations are added to the previously learned PACT components of purpose and audience. For example, the overall purpose may be to inform, influence, inspire, or instruct, and beyond that you may have clearly delineated specific objectives. However, you must now consider why multimedia would be effective. Is it appropriate? What specific purpose will it serve? Is there another option that might be more effective (and less costly)? If your presentation is highly interactive and you plan to deliver it via the Web, scalability becomes important. That is, as more and more people access your Web site, will your software and hardware be capable of handling the additional traffic without slow-downs, erratic behavior in terms of search functions, etc.? You must select team members who are capable of scaling up with your project and of implementing systems that will allow for this.

Audience analysis also takes on additional dimensions especially if your multimedia is user-facilitated. The use of multimedia should enhance the audience's experience, including the individual user if it is a user-facilitated presentation. If there is no need for interactivity, then you should ask yourself whether a simple videotape or linear presentation would do the job just as well. Additionally, there are content issues that must be considered; these are discussed next.

Additional Content Considerations

While this chapter encompasses multimedia as a presentation technique (the T in PACT), it is important to discuss the additional content issues that accompany this powerful technique.

Concept Development

The *concept* of your presentation represents your overall vision. It could be a simple statement that helps keep the presentation focused, or it could be a metaphor. Your concept helps guide the development process. When you add more detail and notes on how your concept can be achieved, it becomes a *treatment*. Sometimes, you will hear the words "concept" and "treatment" used interchangeably.

One informing and instructing presentation to teach kids how to use 9-1-1 created by Creative Media Solutions used the concept of a children's television crew headquartered in their parents' garage. The crew went "on location" to learn about emergency medical services, visiting local fire stations and interviewing paramedics, etc. That simple concept helped to guide the presentation of the content (i.e., in the context of a homey TV studio), how the child actors would interact (i.e., as reporters, producers, etc.), and many of the production techniques that were used. The concept grew into a treatment that, once approved by the client, was developed into a complete *script*.

The script includes all the text, visuals, narration (if any) and other audio requirements, and interactive components. The concept, as you will see, is closely related to the *interface design* of your project, which is discussed after another content consideration, *information design*.

Information Design

Information design in multimedia is related to the content component of PACT. In chapter 4, you were introduced to a variety of ways of organizing content using TOP ACT: Topic, Order (Alphabetical, Continuum, and Time), and Position. Information design incorporates techniques that make the structure of information within a multimedia presentation more apparent, clear, and useful.

Have you ever looked at a multimedia product and felt as if you were experiencing information overload? Perhaps the information was just too dense, or there was too much information on one screen. Good information design should help eliminate that experience by arranging the content in a logical, organized fashion. Using TOP ACT, let's say the content of your user-facilitated multimedia presentation is organized by topics; the major topics might utilize color-coded menu buttons as a way of quickly and easily associating subtopics and primary topics. A user could easily link to a subtopic, if desired, thus eliminating the problem of information overload. Remember, there is often more than one logical way to organize your information; good information designers may incorporate a number of ways for users to view the information they desire.

> *The wider our horizons and the more powerful our technology, the greater we have come to value the individual.*
>
> John Naisbitt & Patricia Aburdene, 16-17

Interface Design

While information design is more concerned with the information architecture or structure, the interface of a multimedia presentation is also focused on its look and feel. Information design thus contributes to the overall interface.

Building the interface is closely tied to realizing the concept of the presentation. For example, if the concept involves teaching the planetary system through creating a spaceship to travel through space, then the interface might resemble the control panel of a spaceship. The user, of course, is the captain of his or her ship. The screen layout could include high-tech panels, switches, and fader bars, each with a different but obvious function. A communications screen could display the learning modules. Navigating to each module would be easy and intuitive. Spacey-sounding audio cues could inform users of what information they have already retrieved. Interactive opportunities could abound with one being an intergalactic challenge (i.e., quiz) to test the user's knowledge of each planetary system explored.

Interface design includes the screen layout, menus, navigation aids, help systems, everything that contributes to your audience's interactive experience. Consistency is important in designing an interface. All navigational buttons and other cues should remain consistent throughout the presentation to reduce possible confusion. A good interface is seamless to users. They shouldn't have to think about it or how to accomplish something; it should simply be intuitive.

Content/Design Documentation

A number of design documents relate to your content. First, there is your detailed script which evolved from your concept. In addition to describing the visual design, audio and narration, musical elements and sound effects, text, and animations, it also describes the nature of the interactivity that can be expected in the various parts of your presentation. Sample user interactions, for example, would be depicted with more detailed descriptions of possible interactive scenarios saved for other documents as described below. Storyboards or illustrated plans of your multimedia presentation are helpful in roughing out the visual design and overall interface of your project.

If this were a more sophisticated presentation than what can be accomplished with presentation software, you will also need a document that can be used by the programmer(s) to specify the structure and interactive components of your presentation. The detailed script along with flowcharts will be useful.

A basic flowchart can visually demonstrate the overall flow or sequence of your presentation to those who will be working on your team or to your prospective clients. These are helpful at the beginning of a project. A higher-level flowchart will show the organization of all the parts of your presentation even showing where interactions can occur. Flowcharts at this level are intended to depict the specific mechanics of each aspect of the multimedia presentation to the programmer(s).

Flowcharts utilize different shaped boxes with text connected by lines to indicate the direction of the interaction. For example, instructing multimedia presentations generally use a diamond-shaped icon to indicate a question followed by several possible answers.

An example of a simple overview flowchart for a user-facilitated informing presentation is presented below. Look for a good flowcharting application that can help you describe your overall presentation structure and expected software behaviors for database searches and interactive components. Most good Web development tools include a flowchart component that displays a hierarchy of your Web pages but these are also helpful to check your work *during* development (as opposed to the design phase).

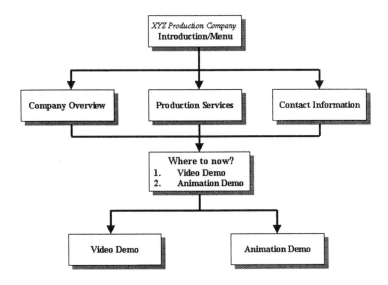

Figure 9.1. Example of a flowchart

From Multimedia Design to Development

After completion of all the design tasks, you are ready to tackle the actual development process. This involves creating all the individual components that will comprise your presentation and then assembling them using any one of a number of software development tools that exist for that purpose. On the basic end, there are current programs like PowerPoint and Persuasion which make creating simple presentations that incorporate multimedia easy to develop. More sophisticated tools include Flash, Authorware, Macromedia Director, and a score of others. If you are developing a Web site, there are many additional tools at your disposal and, of course, there is the option of custom programming, as well.

Let's assume you are putting together a PowerPoint presentation. Although the program provides some graphics tools, you will most likely need to import graphics, videos, photos, music, animations, and other elements into your presentation. While you might compile the entire presentation yourself, you have previously determined whether you also require the services of others to accomplish certain tasks such as video production, graphics, photography, writing, animation, etc. Earlier, we discussed the various roles of team members. All will use their expertise and a development tool specific to their discipline to create their aspect of the total presentation. Before entering the development or what is often called the production phase, meet again with everyone on your team to ensure that each one is on the same page in terms of your project goals and that each is ready to take the leap from design to development.

While exploring the production tasks related to each potential multimedia component is beyond the scope of this brief chapter, in the paragraphs that follow, we will look at some of the tasks involved in one of the key multimedia areas, that of video and audio. Imagine that at the very same time the video process is taking place, other multimedia components like animation and graphics development will likely be under way, as well. While this example may be at a more advanced level than the multimedia presentation you may be asked to prepare, it provides an excellent primer for all of the tasks involved in creating your multimedia presentation.

Pre-Production

Video production actually begins with production planning or *pre-production*. When planning a video shoot, for example, it is generally necessary to pre-interview the subjects you will be videotaping, location scout, arrange for production dates, talent, etc. We will look at a sample scenario, one that is typical for a Creative Media Solutions production.

This pre-production example involves preparation for a series of video testimonials for inclusion in a college recruitment Web site. The first thing we did was schedule a project *start-up meeting* with the client, in this case, the advertising agency that represented the college. During this meeting, we discussed the overall purpose of the client's Web site and how the video testimonials fit in. The purpose was to recruit prospective students (an *influencing* presentation), and the video testimonials would include current and past students, faculty, and others who could paint a picture of college life and the many resources and opportunities available to would-be students. We also went over the concept, expectations, and a possible shooting plan.

Later, we pre-interviewed candidates for the video testimonials, selecting the most convincing ones for videotaping. We also prepared releases for any on-camera talent, granting permission to use his/her face and voice in the video (it's always a good idea to have a legal counsel review your release forms to make sure everything necessary is covered). Visiting the college and scouting a number of possible locations that would be good for videotaping was yet another pre-production task. With all the necessary research complete, a final preparatory step was creating a *shooting or production plan* that mapped out where we would be taping, dates and times, who was involved (including contact info), etc. As a project manager, you will save valuable time and costs by putting more effort into pre-production. Without ample preparation, you can find yourself having to wing it during the more costly production stage.

Production

Video field production involves videotaping "on location" as opposed to in a studio. On the college production mentioned above, our crew (videographer, sound person, producer, and production assistant) videotaped at a variety of locations on the college campus in addition to areas in the vicinity of the college to demonstrate lifestyle opportunities. Our careful preparation resulted in a smooth shoot: release forms for video participants were ready to sign, our producer knew how long we could spend at each location based on the production plan, and so on.

Studio tapings require the same amount of preparation. The 9-1-1 video mentioned earlier in this chapter was taped in a studio. The set was built to resemble a makeshift child's television studio housed in a garage. A studio environment was selected to provide more control over the situation in terms of lighting, special effects, etc. There are trade-offs, of course; shooting in the field often results in getting great video or unexpected but interesting shots!

Whether in the field or in the studio, it is important that someone take good notes about what shots were acquired, which ones were the good takes (often referred to as the *buy takes*), and timings or the length of the shots or interview segments. Something called *timecode* is recorded alongside the video; this is a handy reference that tells you the placement of the shot on the record media according to hours, minutes, seconds, and frames. (A video frame is one-thirtieth of a second so you can be very precise!)

Another important element of note-taking is tracking the *continuity*. For example, if your main spokesperson is wearing a tie in the first shot of a particular scene, takes it off during a production break, then doesn't replace it for the second shot in the same scene, it will appear disjointed when you edit the two scenes together later in the post-production phase. This is the job of a *script supervisor* on commercial, television program, and film shoots. It saves valuable time in post-production and often costly re-shoots.

Post-Production

Post-production includes editing your audio and video onto a timeline that helps you organize your video clips on multiple tracks using time-code. Here you provide the sequence of shots for your video piece, and add music and sweetening (e.g., sound effects), transitions, and other special effects. There are numerous applications on the market for digitally editing video and audio.

One of the first post-production tasks is carefully scrutinizing the video that was taped in the field. This process, called *logging*, involves noting the best shots for your needs, their length, source (e.g., the number of the tape or record media if you used multiple ones during your shoot), and how well they will work with other shots you wish to include. You will use the script that was written in the design phase as your guide. The end product of this task is an *edit decision list* (EDL) that describes each of your clips, their timecode, duration, and location in terms of the source media. With the EDL and your final video script, you are ready to edit the video portions of your presentation.

An editor is the person who will then capture the selected shots into the computer (that could also be you if you know how!). At this point, it will greatly assist you later in the process if you carefully label your shots now. Devise a system that will help you easily identify the contents of each video and audio file.

Because video is such a space hog on the computer, another post-production consideration that comes into play when you are producing multimedia for the Web is *file size*. For example, with some of the video that we captured for the college testimonials, we decided to keep the audio portion only. That is, we used the editing program to remove the video portion and keep just the audio or what is sometimes referred to as the "sound-bite." By stripping the video and keeping only the audio, the file size was greatly reduced. This helped speed up the loading of the files for users who did not yet have the benefit of high speed Internet connections. To make it more interesting (and in order to identify the speaker), we placed a small still picture of the individual above the sound-bite. Because these were interviews, sometimes referred to as "talking heads," the lack of motion was an acceptable trade-off for reduced file size and increased speed.

Think About

As you read this section you may have thought, "I'm never going to have to do this. I'll probably purchase existing video, use public domain video, or outsource any video production." Regardless, if you use video in your multimedia presentation, it is important to think about all of the aspects of video production and post-production so that you can make the best and most cost-effective decisions possible.

Delivery

If all you were going to do was produce a video for use on its own (as in a tape or other media with large storage capacity), you would not have to worry about compression. However, when your videos are incorporated into a multimedia presentation for a delivery system where space and loading time are at a premium (e.g., Web delivery), *compression* is important. It is a way to encode your video and audio so that it takes up much less space than in its original form. There are many different compression formats, and each has its advantages and disadvantages with regard to image quality, compressed size, and performance in terms of motion. We would like to think that by the time this text is available we won't need to worry about such things because the speed of all possible delivery media and Internet access speed will be an issue of the past; but that is probably wishful thinking for the near future.

Our discussion above was confined to video and audio production. Remember, that at the same time the video is being produced, you may have other team members working on other aspects of your project. The animator may be designing a logo or titles for the presentation, while your graphic artist could be creating a logo or titles for your presentation, and so on. With all your elements produced, you can begin assembling your presentation.

Programming

If you are using PowerPoint to facilitate a presentation you are giving to an audience in your organization, most likely you can put together your own presentation by assembling all the elements yourself. However, if your presentation is a stand-alone digital product or a sophisticated informational Web site, chances are you will require the assistance of a programmer. Some projects may be developed with high-level scripting languages or authoring systems that simplify this task substantially; others may require at least some custom programming.

Projects that incorporate extensive information databases will likely require a database expert. As mentioned earlier, flowcharts, clear scripts, etc. will greatly help the programmer and reduce time. Also, prior or continued prototype development will contribute to the clarification of tasks required of the programmer.

Even with all the preparation, expect programming to take even longer than you planned as it generally does. What does that mean? Increase your contingency budget if you can!

Communicating with the Programmers

Your planning and preparation will be critical at this point. You can save valuable time and expenditures by providing detailed instructions to programmers through storyboards, flowcharts, etc.

Setting *validation criteria* will be important especially for larger projects. This is something you start at the beginning of a project and refine as the project progresses since new features may be added in the process. A validation test or script should contain all the components and functionalities of your multimedia presentation or product, paying special attention to things that could go wrong. For example, what are the expected behaviors of a particular search that a user might initiate? The programmer can utilize such a document to test the progress of his or her coding and in *alpha testing*. Alpha-testing is the first round of tests, usually conducted in-house to test functionality and correct any errors that are demonstrated.

—Presentation Tip—

If you are doing your own programming, make sure you do NOT rely on only yourself for testing. Have others test your code regularly!

schedule and the budget is critical, you may have to consider trade-offs. Can you accomplish the same goals with a slightly less costly production technique? Can you streamline your programming requirements without compromising overall quality? Can you reduce your graphics requirements and still keep your multimedia presentation engaging and motivating? Because you really do not want to have to be faced with making too many trade-offs late in your development process, it is critical to establish a realistic budget and timeline at the beginning of the process. Keep in mind Taylor's value-added factors when deciding exactly what content and techniques to use. Then, your good communications skills, motivational strategies, management, and clear vision will help you stay on target as best as possible.

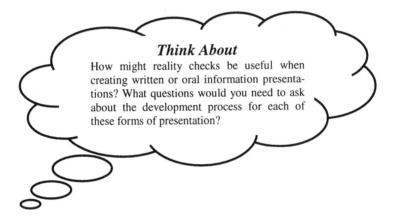

Think About

How might reality checks be useful when creating written or oral information presentations? What questions would you need to ask about the development process for each of these forms of presentation?

Evaluation

In a previous section, we mentioned that alpha-testing was generally conducted in-house. Later, you should also *beta-test* your presentation. Beta-testing is generally conducted with representatives from your target audience. Allow them to go through the process and identify problems and inconsistencies. Make sure you have developed an easy-to-use form that your testers can fill out, allowing space for comments. Also, include a section on your form for identifying information not only about the individual tester, but also the details about the computer speed, software/browser versions, etc. that might account for certain results on the test. In one of our tests, we determined that a browser used by several of our testers just wouldn't function correctly with our software. Either we had to correct our software to be compatible with that browser or we had to inform users that the one browser was not optimal for use with our presentation. At the time of the publication of this book, we were still considering this one! In any event, the reason for beta-testing is to identify errors and accurately communicate them to the programmer(s) so that corrections or modifications can be made.

You don't have to wait until your presentation is completely developed to beta-test. Get reactions from your potential audience along the way. Solicit their suggestions for improvement. This is true for any mode of presentation whether it is automated, presenter-facilitated, or user-facilitated.

One of the projects undertaken by Creative Media Solutions and the co-authors of this text involved setting up a Research Management Site (RMS) from which potential users would visit the prototype Web site and then return to the RMS to engage in threaded discussions in an online asynchronous focus group, as well as answer online questionnaires. (This project is described more fully in the next section of this chapter.)

If you are developing a Web site as your presentation mode, ask yourself questions like the following throughout the development process:

- Have you given your audience enough baseline information to support the content you are presenting?
- Is your Web site presented in a stimulating and interesting way?
- Is the interface engaging?
- Is the content meaningful to your audience?
- Are there activities on your site that add value?
- Is your site well organized with a logical structure to the information presented?
- Is it easy to use?
- Does everything function the way it should?
- Are the searches fast enough?

The above questions form the basis of the business-related Web site evaluation instruments included in the next chapter in our discussion of different ways to evaluate presentations of all types.

Bringing It All Together: A Web-Based Multimedia Project

A Web-based project, encompassing all of the multimedia functions described in this chapter, was undertaken by Creative Media Solutions under the direction of the authors of this book. It was called *S.O.S. for Information Literacy* and was funded by the U.S. Department of Education. The project was directed toward classroom teachers and school librarians and provided numerous strategies, lesson plans, videos, etc., designed to enhance their teaching of information skills to children in the elementary grades. Figure 9.2 shows a screen-capture of the top portion of the homepage illustrating the interface design. Notice the hook just under the banner: "Welcome to *S.O.S. for Information Literacy*, a virtual idea factory for educators teaching information skills to children in grades K-5!" It captures the targeted user's attention by promising to deliver something this audience is always looking for— new ideas for teaching information skills. The banner itself is designed to capture the global essence of information literacy and the power that information literacy offers to its children.

The information design aspect of the project was simple. It used a topical organization approach. Each menu option from *Strategies* to *Topic Search* actually represented a searchable database. The menu buttons, which had a gold diagonal border surrounding them, would change color and tilt in the opposite direction when passed over by the mouse. When selected, the menu button of the specific page the user was visiting would remain highlighted in blue. The homepage featured a teaser, as well, called *In the Spotlight*, which encouraged users to visit the Spotlight page and discover an interesting project undertaken by one of their peers in the education field.

The project required over thirty data tables, hundreds of data relationships, and a client server interface as well as a Web interface. Several database experts were responsible for this aspect of the project.

Video production was intensive and involved all video preproduction, production, and post-production tasks outlined earlier in this chapter. Because the Web was the delivery system, we also encountered space and loading time issues. Videos were scaled to a small but viewable size and were greatly compressed to reduce file size and loading time on the part of the user. At the time of the printing of this text, these were still important issues to consider although they will become less important as technology and access to that technology improves.

Many people comprised the project team, from researchers to programmers. Communication was a critical component of the project. The principal investigator had to make sure that each person had the right vision and that the team remained on target both in terms of that vision and the timeline, which had little room for slippage. That meant those *reality checks* along the way were very important!

Finally, as mentioned earlier, evaluation using the RMS site and a focus group helped keep the project doing what it was intended to do, i.e., meeting the needs of its target audience—educators.

Let's Hear It! ⑴ 🝰

Tom Hardy is President and CEO of Grant Systems, Inc. located in Ithaca, New York. The company has created numerous information systems including database-driven Web sites for a wide variety of corporate clients. Tom described a Web-based project his company had undertaken for a client in the public relations industry headquartered in Washington, D.C. Grant Systems had been commissioned to create a Web site that not only described his client's services but also provided essential information to site visitors, including news on political issues on a state-by-state basis. This involved the development of searchable databases and a means of quickly updating the data. The site, as the client envisioned it, was primarily text-based with useful searchable databases and some graphics sprinkled here and there, but no audio or video. Grant Systems did an excellent job of developing an information-rich site, but they wanted to do more. A client presentation was in order.

"Before describing the presentation, I should provide some background information about the project and client my company was working with," Tom explained. "One of the most difficult parts of the project had been working with various staff members at the firm and dealing with multiple input. Everyone had a suggestion and they were all different."

"At one of the first meetings," Tom continued, "some of the staff members had contributed ideas for the *interface* and had sketched them out on large *storyboard* forms. It looked cluttered and confusing, kind of 'hodge podge.' It was, of course, helpful in demonstrating points that the different departments thought should be included. I acknowledged the value of their efforts and then gently started exploring some other options for displaying the information and for the general look and feel of the site. The point is, a client presentation requires people skills as well as technical knowledge. After absorbing all the input (and more) than was needed, we agreed on one individual taking the lead on the client side and all information would be filtered through him."

Even before the presentation, you can see that Tom had paid special attention to his *audience*. Those first meetings were critical in developing a product that addressed all his client's needs and concerns. It was also important to establish a client relationship based upon mutual understanding and confidence. As the *project manager*, Tom had to carefully communicate all expectations to his project team. Grant Systems spent a lot of time on *information design* and management. They wanted the user to access the information in a flexible and useful way. The *interface* they designed was attractive, effective, and easy to navigate. Now it was time to present the final product.

The presentation was delivered on site in the client's conference room. All the staffers that had contributed input and the managers were present. This *presenter-facilitated presentation* consisted of about six PowerPoint slides highlighting what the client had requested and what had been accomplished (a kind of progress report), and included a link to the actual Web site for an online demonstration of the product.

Tom encouraged his audience to ask questions during the demonstration. He received input on several additions that individuals thought would enhance the site, fueled by their general enthusiasm for what they saw. They commented on Grant Systems' seamless interface and what an improvement it was over the initial suggestions. His excellent presentation skills helped to create an environment in which his audience felt respected for their previous contributions to the project as well as to the design changes that Tom had initiated. But there was more to this presentation than simply a progress report (*informing* presentation), or client feedback. Tom's other broad purpose was to *influence* his audience to add several new features to the site.

"The presentation was going along smoothly and I had addressed most of their concerns and ideas," Tom stated. "What I couldn't answer on the spot, I told them I would discuss with my programmers and get back to them. What I also wanted to do was validate that the addition of video and audio elements to the site would be an enhancement. So prior to the presentation, I had my production staff compile a sample video and audio segment. The video segment showed shots of Washington, D.C., their location, offices, etc. something I had captured on a previous visit. The professional narration and music really made it shine. Then, I had an example of a customer testimonial. When I showed this during the presentation, it got everyone's attention and most agreed that it would be a good idea to pursue. I left feeling very good about this one."

As an endnote, Tom did enhance the site with audio, video, and additional graphics. He attributes the success of his multimedia presentation (both informing and influencing) to thorough *planning* and *preparation* and carefully *listening to his audience* throughout the process that culminated in this presentation.

Enhancing DD Inc.'s Web Site

Jacqueline Cooper, Director of Information Technology (IT), and Dan Bernstein, Marketing Director, at DD Inc. have been asked to look into the possibility of producing several videos for DD Inc.'s Web site. During a recent staff meeting in which Deborah Garcia had asked for creative input to enhance the Web site, there was agreement that introducing potential customers to DD Inc.'s team of denim designers might be a good idea. So Jacqueline and Dan, with some of their staff, will form a multimedia design team to create a video component for the DD Inc. Web site.

Learning Check

1. What is multimedia?

2. There are several uses of multimedia that pertain to presentations:

    *   Which type is presented in a linear format with no interactivity and no speaker support?
    *   Which type supports or reinforces what the speaker/presenter is saying?
    *   In which type of multimedia presentation does the *user* have control of pacing, content selection, and opportunities for interactivity?

3. Is multimedia always appropriate? If not, when would it be least effective?

4. Name several upfront considerations that are important when planning multimedia presentations?

5. What is meant by "repurposing" and how can it help the bottom line?

6. What is it important to acquire when using outside sources of material for your multimedia presentation?

7. What is one of the most important functions of the project manager?

8. What is a "prototype" and how is it used in developing multimedia?

9. Describe two additional dimensions of the content component of PACT that are associated with multimedia presentations.

10. What is the difference between *alpha* and *beta* testing?

Do & Discuss

Jacqueline Cooper and Dan Bernstein have been assigned to produce several videos for DD Inc.'s Web site, introducing visitors to some of DD Inc.'s denim designers through mini-biographies of their lives and careers.

- What are some of the pre-production tasks they need to consider?
- If the interviews they have videotaped are excellent but run a bit long, what are some of the things they could do?
- What benefit do you see in incorporating the designer interviews with the Web site? What purpose (think of the four Is) would *you* want them to serve? With your purpose in mind, what questions might you ask the designers to answer that would help serve your purpose?
- What other types of video clips do you think would increase the value and appeal of DD Inc.'s Web site?
- What will be the management responsibilities for this project and how do you think Jacqueline and Dan should assign them? Should anyone else from DD Inc. be involved in the project?

Create a basic flowchart to demonstrate the organization of your hypothetical company's multimedia Web site.

Coming Up...

In this chapter, you were introduced to a number of concepts and issues related to designing and developing multimedia presentations. We also introduced the topic of evaluation and the importance of setting validation criteria for complex multimedia projects. Evaluation is an important topic and we dedicate an entire chapter to it coming up next!

Sources of Quotes

Naisbitt, John, and Patricia Aburdene. *Megatrends 2000*. New York: William Morrow & Company, Inc., 1990.

Shneiderman, Ben. *Designing the User Interface: Strategies for Effective Human-Computer Interaction*, 2nd ed., Reading, Mass.: Addison-Wesley Publishing Company, Inc., 1993.

Chapter 10

Evaluating Your Presentation

After you have delivered your information presentation, how will you know you have achieved your purpose? How will you know you have met the information needs of your audience? How will you know if you have selected and organized your content in an effective manner? How will you know if your technique was the best method for delivering your content? In other words, how do you know how you did? The answer to all of these questions is—EVALUATION!

Objectives

By the end of chapter 10, you will:

- understand the difference between a formative and a summative evaluation and know when to use each,
- understand how to conduct a focus group to formatively evaluate a presentation,
- be able to design a rubric for summatively evaluating a presentation,
- know when a follow-up evaluation is appropriate, and
- understand the unique requirements for evaluating Web sites, using the *WebSite Motivational Analysis Checklist*.

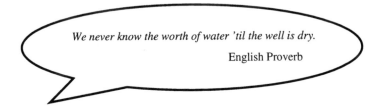

We never know the worth of water 'til the well is dry.

English Proverb

What Is Evaluation?

Evaluation requires the collection, organization, analysis, and reporting of assessment data. An evaluation determines the ability of your presentation to accomplish your purpose, meet the needs of your audience, and determine the quality of your content and the effectiveness of your technique (including use of media and support materials).

A well-planned and well-conducted evaluation can provide useful evidence of:

- the worth of a presentation,
- how to improve future presentations, and
- justification for funding/support for current or future presentations.

You may need to design any or all of the following types of evaluations:

- *Formative Evaluation:* This takes place before or during the presentation. The results can be used to modify the presentation while it is being developed and/or conducted.
- *Summative Evaluation:* This takes place immediately after the presentation has been delivered. The results help you assess how well the presentation has achieved its purpose and whether it has met your objectives and the needs of your audience.
- *Follow-Up Evaluation:* This takes place at some point or points after the presentation has been received. The results help you determine the long-term impact of the presentation.

Think About

As you read about the different methods for evaluating presentations, think about which ones you may have completed at presentations you have read, viewed, or attended. Were any types more useful than others for expressing your opinions about the presentation?

Dress Rehearsal: Formative Evaluation

Formative evaluation (sometimes referred to as a pilot test or usability test) provides feedback data on the effectiveness of all aspects of a presentation in order to revise that presentation *before* it is delivered to its intended audience (or, in the case of oral presentations, even while it is in progress). It generally employs less formal methods than a summative evaluation. Perhaps the easiest, quickest, and most meaningful way to get useful feedback on how to improve your presentation before you deliver it is to use one of the following approaches.

Focus Groups

The focus group is one of the most common approaches to gathering information for a formative evaluation. Focus groups are a common method for gaining feedback concerning any type of creation from a product to a presentation. They have been used by such varied groups as software producers to test the usability of a new product, by advertising agencies to assess the effectiveness of a proposed advertising campaign, and by politicians to judge the response to their campaign platform.

To conduct a focus group:

1. *Gather a small group of three to five people who have characteristics similar to your target audience.* For example, if your oral presentation is to be delivered to your IT department, find some other IT professionals to participate in your formative evaluation. If your technical report is to be presented to your stockholders, find a few people that share similar backgrounds with the target audience to read and critique your report.

2. *Deliver the presentation as similarly as possible to how the actual presentation will be presented.* You may not be able to perfectly simulate your presentation environment, but you should try to create as similar a situation as possible. For example, if you are giving an oral presentation in an auditorium, find a large meeting room or, if possible, go to the actual auditorium to pilot test your presentation. If you are creating a Web site, ask your participants to access the test site from the probable access location of your target audience (e.g., home, office, lab).

3. *Ask participants to write down reactions, comments, suggestions, and ideas regarding any or all aspects of your presentation.* For example, participants should provide feedback regarding:

- how smoothly your content flows,
- whether the level of content is too easy, too difficult, or just right,
- whether the content selected for presentation is appropriate, relevant, and understandable,
- if the presentation captures attention and maintains interest throughout,
- the technical quality of the presentation (e.g., visually clear, clear sound, grammatical correctness, appropriate volume, etc.),
- length of time to complete the presentation, and
- ways to improve the presentation.

4. Revise your presentation, as necessary.

Flashback

Does the focus group approach remind you of something else you have read in this book? This evaluation method is something like the beta testing approach used to formatively evaluate multimedia presentations by allowing the target audience to go through the process and identify problems and inconsistencies.

Other Formative Evaluation Methods

There are several other methods for collecting formative evaluation information. They are written feedback, discussion, one-on-one, and videotaping.

Written Feedback. A more formal (and anonymous) means of collecting formative data than those below, the written feedback form allows you to collect information *while your presentation is actually in progress*. Open-ended questions that allow a broader expression of opinion tend to be the most useful. Make sure audience members do not put their names on the form (this will guarantee more frank and candid opinions).

Discussion. This method can be used *during* an oral presentation, particularly long presentations like workshops or seminars. It is possible to collect information through informal discussions with all or part of your audience about the effectiveness of your presentation while it is in progress and, where possible, modify it as you proceed. For example, you may discover that your audience really likes the examples you have been providing and want more of them. You can then add more examples. Or, your audience might reveal that they find the group exercises you are using are too time-consuming and they just want to get the information. That way you can cut back on the exercises and either provide more in-depth information or more time for questions about the content.

One-on-one. This method is particularly useful for formatively evaluating written or multimedia presentations. For this type of evaluation, the presenter sits with the participant and observes as he/she proceeds through the presentation. Often the participant is asked to "talk-aloud," expressing his/her thoughts, need for clarification, reactions, etc. while the observer records the talk-aloud comments. The comments are then used by the presentation creator to determine what changes and modifications should be made.

Videotaping. This method is particularly useful for formatively evaluating oral presentations. Videotaping yourself as you deliver an oral presentation (either alone or in front of your focus group) will allow you to identify behaviors you want to add (e.g., more smiling) or eliminate (e.g., less throat clearing).

Flashback

Remember those unwanted personal mannerisms described in chapter 8? Can you see how videotaping your presentation ahead of time can help you identify (and eliminate) these annoying behaviors?

Your Final Answer: Summative Evaluation

A summative evaluation is conducted once the presentation has been fully developed and delivered. It permits conclusions about the effectiveness, value, and efficiency of the various aspects of the content and delivery technique. The results may also be used to help make decisions about whether the presentation should be repeated or delivered to a broader or different audience; if so, the evaluation is also formative in some respects, as it might allow you to make some important changes before more widespread implementation.

Summative Evaluation Methods

There are several methods for collecting data about your presentation once it has been received by your audience. Surveys and questionnaires are the most common approaches for gathering information for a summative evaluation. They are particularly useful for large and/or distributed audiences but can be effective methods for collecting evaluation data from any size group. For example, a workshop for other professionals in your field may require a type of written survey that participants complete at the end of the workshop. An online training program may use an electronic questionnaire to collect summative data on its effectiveness after the training has been completed.

Surveys and questionnaires can be designed using any or all of the following formats:

Multiple Choice

Multiple choice items may take the form of a question with a choice of four to five responses *or* a statement stem with a choice of four to five endings. Examples of these two types of multiple choice items are:

Multiple Choice Question: How interesting was this presentation to you? __ a. very interesting __ b. interesting __ c. somewhat interesting __ d. not interesting	Multiple Choice Statement: The content of this presentation was: __ a. very relevant to me __ b. relevant to me __ c. somewhat relevant to me __ d. not relevant to me

Checklists

Checklists are a quick and easy way to assess presentation performance. Participants are presented with a list of statements or questions
for which they indicate whether or not certain elements are present or
absent. A comments column allows more information and explanation
to be provided. Here is an excerpt from a presentation evaluation
checklist:

ITEM	YES	NO	COMMENTS
This presentation was interesting.			
This presentation was relevant.			

Likert-Type Scales

Likert-type scales typically allow participants to describe along a numerical continuum the degree to which a presentation meets performance criteria. This method allows you to collect more precise quantitative evaluation data. Here are some examples of Likert-type items:

> This presentation was:
> *Very interesting*   *Not interesting*
> 10 9   8   7   6   5   4   3   2   1
>
> *Very relevant*   *Not relevant*
> 10 9   8   7   6   5   4   3   2   1

Open-Ended Questions

Sometimes it is important to let your audience respond to questions in a
narrative or anecdotal way where they can express themselves in their
own words, rather than choosing pre-designed responses. Open-ended
questions target issues for which you want or need more information or
clarification. You need to allow sufficient space for responses of varying lengths. Here is an example:

> Describe ways in which the presenter made this
> presentation interesting to you.
>
>
> In what ways was this presentation relevant to you?

Rubrics

A rubric is a rating system by which presenters determine different, clearly defined levels of performance effectiveness for each aspect of the presentation. A rubric can by used by (1) the presentation audience to assess the quality of the presentation and/or (2) the presenter as a self-assessment tool for reflecting on the quality of the presentation and learning from his/her successes and failures.

To develop a rubric:

- List the important aspects of the presentation.
- Define a limited number of performance criteria (the most important).
- Clearly and simply define performance criteria in terms of observable presentation behaviors or characteristics.

On the following page is an example of a simple oral presentation rubric based on the PACT Model. This rubric only provides general assessment categories and a few possible presentation skills. (We were constrained by space limitations in our presentation of it to you.) If we were to fully develop this rubric, we would need to go into more depth, including many more categories of items (e.g., Technical Aspects, Power Point Skills) and more specific items (e.g., Citations and References, Pacing, Handouts).

PRESEN- TATION SKILLS				SCORE	COMMENTS
Purpose	Stated clearly & sustained throughout presentation. 5	Adequate explanation but some materials questionably relevant. 4 3 2	Connection to materials presented and purpose are unclear. 1		
Audience	Engaged and interactive. Materials appropriate. 5	Adequate amount of attention & involvement. Most materials appropriate. 4 3 2	Lost or distracted with information presented. 1		
Content	Exceptional selection & organization. Information correct, concise, credible, clear. 5	Information generally accurate and relevant. 4 3 2	Factual accuracy & relevance of information questionable. 1		
Technique	Presenters meet needs of audience and make effective use of: voice, eye contact, movement, gestures, tone & enthusiasm. 5	Presenters use physical presentation skills adequately. 4 3 2	Problems are evident with physical skills, such as: poor voice projection, lack of eye contact or distracting movements. 1		
			TOTAL SCORE:		

Back for More: Follow-Up Evaluation

Evaluating your presentation after some time has elapsed since it was received may be the best measure of a presentation's real impact. The information you gather can also be used to make further improvements or as additional evidence for future support. The downside is that follow-up evaluation can be costly, both in terms of money and time. Before you plan a follow-up evaluation, you may want to think about its cost-effectiveness and usefulness.

Follow-up studies can take several forms. You can send questionnaires to your participants to find out how useful the information presented has been to them in their particular context. In some cases, you may want to visit participants at their site for observations or interviews either to identify changes in participants' behaviors or to discuss various aspects of the presentation's effectiveness (or lack thereof). However, while open-ended questions may provide the most and best information to the presenter, more quantitative information provided by such methods as Likert-type scales is important for demonstrating impact in order to justify continuing support from a boss or client.

We focus the next section of this chapter on the evaluation of a specific technique—the multimedia Web site.

Evaluating Web Sites

Millions of people worldwide are seeking information by searching and surfing the Internet, looking for needed products and services, or just exploring to see what's out there. As a result, businesses want to know if their Web sites are attracting both searchers and surfers, interesting them long enough to search their sites thoroughly, and motivating them to purchase their product or service. At the same time, they hope that people will frequently return to their site and/or "spread the word" to others. As the number of commercial Web sites continues to grow at an astounding rate, the competitive market requires effective interface design guidelines and evaluation criteria so that Web sites accomplish these goals.

However, summative evaluation of Web sites presents some unique issues. The Web contains simultaneous, integrated multimedia information in ways that have never been possible with other media. Users can access video, text, audio, graphics, interactive components, links to other Web resources, and even live-camera action in one presentation package. As a result of their dynamic, interactive nature, Web site evaluation requires a broader concept of evaluation than used for other information presentation forms such as print or video.

Currently, there are dozens of Web evaluation instruments designed to help educators judge the suitability of a Web site for their instructional needs. Some emphasize content validity issues (such as whether the information is accurate or current), while others target functionality issues (such as whether links are active or buttons work). However, we believe that Web site assessment requires different types of evaluation instruments that represent a broader perspective on evaluation. This broader perspective encompasses both content validity and functionality issues but in the context of another, often ignored, aspect of Web site evaluation—something we call *motivational quality.*[1]

Motivational Quality

Motivational quality refers to those factors that affect whether a person (1) is attracted to a Web site, (2) decides to explore a Web site, and (3) returns to a Web site. Because businesses expect their Web sites to attract both first-time customers and return customers, high motivational quality rating of that Web site becomes an essential goal.

Flashback

In chapter 8 we described the *expectancy-value (E-V) theory* of motivation which states a person's motivation is based on his or her perception that there is something of *value* in a task and that he or she has an *expectancy for the successful* accomplishment of that task.

Applying this theory to the Web environment, a site that *stimulates* the interest and curiosity of the user and provides *meaningful* content and activities may be considered a valuable Web site. Further a Web site that provides an *organized* sequence and placement of content and is *easy to use* should promote a positive *expectancy for success*. The degree to which these qualities are present comprises the *motivational quality* of that Web site. Using the two general evaluation components (value, expectancy for success) and the four sub-components (i.e., is the Web site stimulating, meaningful, organized, and easy to use for the user), we have developed a series of Web evaluation instruments, known collectively as *WebMAC*. We describe these instruments below.

The WebSite Motivational Analysis Checklist (WebMAC)

Based on the components of expectancy-value theory, we created a set of Web evaluation instruments that are intended for use by a wide range of audiences in business and education to assess the Web sites they use. *The Website Motivational Analysis Checklist*© (or *WebMAC*, for short) is comprised of eight individual, easy-to-use instruments, six of which were designed for use in educational contexts while the remaining two were created for use in business contexts.

The *WebMAC* instruments differ from other Web site evaluation instruments in several ways:

- While other instruments are typically expert-centered, the *WebMACs* are user-centered, intended to provide feedback from potential users of the Web site.
- The *WebMACs* are based on a well-known motivation theory applied to the Web environment.
- The *WebMACs* focus on motivational issues from an information perspective.
- The *WebMACs* use a research approach and have been tested and validated by over 800 users worldwide.
- The *WebMACs* incorporate a variety of methods for analysis and interpretive feedback, using a variety of visual scoring mechanisms and grid templates.
- The *WebMACs* may be used to identify areas for improvement of an existing Web site, provide guidance for the design of a new Web site, or allow comparison of multiple Web sites.

Before using these thirty-two item, Likert-type instruments, the evaluator is encouraged to spend time exploring the target Web site in order to have some familiarity with its content and structure. The evaluator records on a scoring sheet his or her agreement ratings for each item on a four-point scale from 0 (strongly disagree) to 3 (strongly agree). The instrument also allows the scorer to use the designation N/A (Not Applicable) when a feature is not present at the Web site. Later, the evaluator must go back and assign a specific score to each N/A item after determining whether the site would have benefited from the missing feature, didn't require it, or was better off without it.

When all scoring is complete, each of the thirty-two items will have a numerical score (sixteen items related to each of the E-V components: value and expectancy for success; eight items for each of the four subcomponents).

Here is an example of each category from *WebMAC E-Commerce*.

Value: Stimulating
    __ 1. The home page of this Web site is eye-catching and visually interesting.

Value: Meaningful
    ___ 6. This Web site provides links to other relevant Web sites.

Expectancy for Success: Organized
____ 11. There is a menu or site map that helps me understand how this Web site is organized.

Expectancy for Success: Easy-to-Use
____ 16. Navigating this Web site does not require any special skills or experience.

The scores are then transferred onto several scoring graphs and grids, allowing quick and easy recognition of areas that are strong in motivational quality and areas in need of improvement. The *WebMAC E-Commerce*[2] and *WebMAC E-Business*[3] evaluation instruments, administration directions, scoring guidelines, and analysis charts are included in their entirety in Appendix B. (Full-size electronic versions of these instruments are available under the "Resources" listing through Syracuse University's Center for Digital Commerce Web site at (http://istweb.syr.edu/~digital).

Let's Hear It! ⑩⌒?

Jill Ann Hurst, President of Hurst Associates, Ltd. located in Fairport, New York, provides us with an example of a presentation she delivered at a one-day conference for local historians held at a hotel in upstate New York. Hurst Associates, Ltd. is a company that provides business intelligence services including business research, knowledge management and intellectual property research. Jill's presentation was intended to give her Audience of more than sixty local historians (mostly volunteers) from various municipalities in New York State an overview of digitization and motivate them to tie into the creation of Web sites for historical societies. As such, we'd call it first an *inspiring* presentation.

Jill started with a *hook* that grabbed everyone's attention—an example of a regional project called *Winning the Vote,* about which she was an expert (having served as project manager). It was an example of both a digitization project and a Web site and its subject matter dealt with women's suffrage in the Rochester, New York area. The project provided her audience with an exciting illustration of how items in a collection can be digitized and used to create an historical Web site.

Jill describes the rest of her presentation's content. "We looked briefly at a couple of other Web sites posted by historical societies in which they had obviously digitized images to include in their Web sites. I then described how one can fund such an effort through grants or one can do this 'on the cheap,' using volunteers and using equipment that people already have." (We think this provided both value and an expectancy for success for her audience). "While the latter method may not result in a Web site of the same quality as something that's heavily funded, it allows them to be able to put up a few images from their collections or from their regions on a historian's Web site." While Jill's presentation contained content that was both interesting and important to her audience, its execution was not without its problems. Read on to find out what happened.

Jill spent a lot of time preparing her presentation. She decided to combine PowerPoint with an oral presentation. Knowing the importance of giving several examples to "whet the appetite" of her audience, she created screen prints of Web sites and other online images which she incorporated into her PowerPoint slides. Why didn't Jill just go live to the Web? "I knew ahead of time that I couldn't go live," she explained. "I had asked about what was available in the room and what they could acquire for me and they couldn't provide Web access. I really didn't want to do overheads. When you talk about things that are on the Internet, there are certain people who would look at it and say 'But you're using *overheads*!'

As it turned out, this would not be the only problem Jill would encounter with her presentation that day. After learning she would not be able to go live to the Web, Jill went to Plan B. "I asked the conference organizer if she could obtain a projection unit for a PowerPoint presentation and she was able to borrow one," she stated. "However, I didn't have access to the projection unit until right before my presentation, so even though I had requested and hoped that they would get the projection equipment a day ahead of time, they didn't. The good news is that before the presentation I was able to take the projection unit out of the room and make sure it worked; the bad news is I couldn't get a sense of what my slides were actually going to look like when I projected them." (Have you guessed where this is going?)

Jill went on, "When you first bring images into PowerPoint, they look fine. But when you project them, oftentimes things get fuzzy. And that's exactly what happened. My intent was not for people to read all the text on the screens but to be able to see the images and get a flavor for how they were laid out and to start thinking about using images to promote their local history." Unfortunately for Jill, at least part of her audience became fixated on the fuzzy words they were trying to read.

What could Jill have done differently? She responded, "I was disappointed that the equipment side didn't turn out as well as I'd hoped. Thinking back, I wish I had imposed on an organization I know that has a projection unit and tried it a week ahead of time. I didn't do that and I really should have, in retrospect. It frustrated some people that they couldn't read the text on my slides."

Like any expert presenter, Jill also had a Plan C which brings us to problem number three. Jill had prepared a set of handouts for her Audience, including copies of the presentation slides and a list of Web sites of historical societies or county historians (the same ones that she had attempted to show in her PowerPoint slides) that they could visit to see how they had used images. "Even though they couldn't get the most out of my screen captures of the images," Jill told us, "they could go on their own and visit the sites directly; that is, if they have Internet access." So Jill sent the master copy of her handouts to the conference organizer asking for copies to be made, assuming that this was a familiar request. As Jill walked up to begin her presentation and reached for her handouts in order to distribute them to her audience, she realized, to her horror, that the handout pages had not been collated! "They had each page (six in all) in a separate pile. We had to hand them out one at a time," Jill recounted painfully. "Then we had to ask 'Does everyone have all six pages?' A couple of people in the audience helped me and we just kinda rolled our eyes at each other."

Despite these problems, Jill's presentation had been a success. "I knew the presentation was well received from the feedback given me by the person who organized the conference and by the questions I got from the audience. My goal, and the goal of the person who asked me to present, was to give this group a flavor of what's possible. It wasn't a training session; it wasn't an in-depth, how-to session. The historians that come to this conference are generally under-funded, under-trained, and they have no historian background, but they're really interested in their local history and helping to preserve it. They probably don't have heavy access to computers either, the type of computers we have access to, the really up-to-date stuff. So it really was giving them ideas for what is possible and how they might do this in cooperation with somebody else cheaply in order to get some images up about their local history." Despite the problems, Jill's presentation certainly accomplished its goal.

What's the Story at DD Inc.?

Alexis Pollanis, DD Inc.'s Director of Human Resources, has instituted a series of training programs for the company's product service employees. She formatively evaluated her training presentation and made appropriate revisions. During the past year, Alexis has delivered the training program to three new groups of product service employees (approximately 20 individuals). She used a rubric to summatively evaluate the training. Now Alexis wants to convert the face-to-face training program to Web-based e-training, incorporating a range of media including photos, videos, graphics, sound, and animations. Before giving Alexis the go-ahead, Deb Garcia, CEO, wants to see evidence of the effectiveness of past training and of the need to expand that training. Alexis must deliver a report to Deb and Sean Fortuno, DD Inc.'s CFO, in about a month.

Learning Check

1. What are the purposes of a presentation evaluation?

2. What are three types of evaluations and when should each be used?

3. What information is provided from a formative evaluation and what are some methods for collecting formative data?

4. What are the steps in conducting a focus group?

5. What are some ways to design items for a survey or questionnaire?

6. What is a rubric?

7. What are the steps for developing a rubric?

8. What is the purpose of a follow-up evaluation?

9. What is the *WebMAC* and what is the motivation theory on which it is based?

10. What are *WebMAC*'s two evaluation components and four sub-components?

Do & Discuss

How should Alexis Pollanis develop her report to her audience (Deb Garcia and Sean Fortuno)?

- What is the purpose of this report?
- What content would be most appropriate to include in her report? How could a follow-up evaluation be used to help her provide the evidence she needs?
- What should her follow-up evaluation plan look like?

The example PACT rubric presented in this chapter is very simple and general. Take the rubric and fully develop it, using what you have learned about effective presentations throughout this book to create relevant sub-items for each of the PACT components. For example, under content you might want to have an item assessing how organized the presentation content is. Test out your rubric with various types of presentations.

Conduct a formative evaluation of chapter 10, using a focus group of three to five people and following the steps described in this chapter.

Develop a rubric for and conduct a summative evaluation of your ViewPoints presentation.

Form groups of five to seven people. Each group member should use the appropriate *WebMAC* instrument to evaluate a commonly designated business Web site. Now compare outcomes across the

Wrapping It Up

In this book we have introduced you to our PACT Model for Effective Information Presentations. Each chapter focused on one of the PACT components: purpose, audience, content, and technique, with the last two spanning several chapters.

We end the book with our *sinker*—a set of exercises that allow you to apply the concepts described throughout this book to five different presentation contexts and evaluate what you have learned. Try them alone or with a group.

What Have You Learned?

Take any or all of the following situations and apply the PACT Model and various concepts in this book, describing how you would design, develop, and evaluate your presentation. Be creative and have fun with them!

Scenario #1

You are assistant director of information systems at a mid-size company that manufactures mini-widgets. Your boss, the director, has decided that it would be useful to install a new email system in the company for everyone on the management level and has asked you to prepare a communication to announce this decision.

- What type(s) of presentations would be appropriate?
- What is the purpose(s) of the presentation(s)?
- Who is your audience(s) and what might you know about them that would help you design your presentation? What factors would be most important to know? How do each of the audience characteristics affect the decisions you make about your presentation?
- How would you organize your content, what content would you include, and how would you find the information you need?
- What technique(s) might you use to present your content?
- How would you evaluate the effectiveness of your presentation?

Scenario #2

The administration of Clinton College has decided to investigate the need for additional computer clusters at the school. You are the IT committee chair at the college. Your committee has recommended twelve classrooms be converted to clusters in various buildings around the campus. Although most of the faculty agrees with the need for these clusters, a small but vocal group strongly opposes the plan. They believe there is already too little classroom space on campus and don't want to give up the twelve classrooms to house "a bunch of machines." The chancellor of Clinton has asked you to present your plan to the entire faculty.

- What type(s) of presentations would be appropriate?
- What is the purpose of the presentation(s)?
- Who is your audience(s) and what might you know about them that would help you design your presentation? What factors would be most important to know? How do each of the audience characteristics affect the decisions you make about your presentation?
- How would you organize your content, what content would you include, and how would you find the information you need?
- What technique(s) might you use to present your content?
- How would you evaluate the effectiveness of your presentation?

Scenario #3

You are the marketing director for a ski resort in Colorado. The resort currently offers all of the usual skiing activities, but the owner wants to attract a wider range of customers to the resort, especially families. Therefore, a wider range of family-type activities and travel packages have been put in place.

- What type(s) of presentations would be appropriate?
- What is the purpose of the presentation(s)?
- Who is your audience(s) and what might you know about them that would help you design your presentation? What factors would be most important to know? How do each of the audience characteristics affect the decisions you make about your presentation?
- How would you organize your content, what content would you include, and how would you find the information you need?
- What technique(s) might you use to present your content?
- How would you evaluate the effectiveness of your presentation?

Scenario #4

You are the information technology consulting team for EasyShop Supermarkets. EasyShop has twenty supermarkets throughout the state. One of your recommendations is to install electronic information kiosks in each store. The kiosks will not only help shoppers locate the items they need but also will give them other important information such as the current price of the item, the ingredients (including calories, sodium level, cholesterol level, fat content, etc.). Before the kiosks are installed, the president of EasyShop has asked you to present the idea to shoppers.

- What type(s) of presentations would be appropriate?
- What is the purpose of the presentation(s)?
- Who is your audience(s) and what might you know about them that would help you design your presentation? What factors would be most important to know? How do each of the audience characteristics affect the decisions you make about your presentation?
- How would you organize your content, what content would you include, and how would you find the information you need?
- What technique(s) might you use to present your content?
- How would you evaluate the effectiveness of your presentation?

Scenario #5

You are a team of information technology consultants hired by the superintendent of the Bayville Public School District to design a technology plan for the schools of Bayville. Bayville is a small town of approximately 4000 people and five schools. The Board of Education has unanimously approved your $2.5 million technology plan for the schools. However, final approval must come from the taxpayers of Bayville who will vote on a referendum to either approve or reject your plan. The mayor has asked you to present the plan to the citizens of Bayville.

- What type(s) of presentations would be appropriate?
- What is the purpose of the presentation(s)?
- Who is your audience(s) and what might you know about them that would help you design your presentation? What factors would be most important to know? How do each of the audience characteristics affect the decisions you make about your presentation?
- How would you organize your content, what content would you include, and how would you find the information you need?
- What technique(s) might you use to present your content?
- How would you evaluate the effectiveness of your presentation?

Notes

1. Ruth V. Small and Marilyn P. Arnone, "Evaluating the Effectiveness of Web Sites," in *Human Centered Methods in Information Systems: Current Research and Practice*, edited by Steven Clarke and B. Le-haney (Hershey, Pa.: Idea Group Publishing, 2000).

2. Ruth V. Small and Marilyn P. Arnone, *The Website Motivational Analysis Checklist (WebMAC): E-Commerce©*. Motivation Mining Co., Fayetteville, N.Y., 2000.

3. Marilyn P. Arnone and Ruth V. Small, *The Website Motivational Analysis Checklist (WebMAC): E-Business©*. Motivation Mining Company, Fayetteville, N.Y., 2000.

Appendix A

Learning Check Answers

Chapter 1

1. Purpose, audience, content, and technique are the four PACT components.

2. Purpose and audience are design components, while content and technique comprise the development components.

3. An organizational identity requires determining an organization's mission and goals, scope, target audience, specific products and/or services, etc.

Chapter 2

1. Four general purposes for presentations are to inform, influence, inspire, and instruct.

2. An inspiring presentation is intended to stimulate an emotional response in your audience.

3. Other terms for an influencing presentation are persuasional or advocacy presentations.

4. Some important situational variables to consider during the presentation planning stage are time of day, location, size of room or presentation space, number of attendees, and available technology.

5. Two critical rules of thumb for planning a presentation are (1) do a background check of your presentation environment and (2) have a back-up plan.

6. Presentation designers also project managers because a presentation is a type of project and the designer must manage the details of designing, developing, delivering, and evaluating a presentation.

7. Some responsibilities of a presentation project manager are managing timeframe, budget, resources, and communication and clarifying the task.

Chapter 3

1. Age range, sex distribution, ethnic mix, group affiliation, group size, and education level are some of the demographic variables that describe an audience.

2. Examples of audience characteristics that can affect how an audience receives a presentation are prior knowledge/experience, cognitive style, personality style, needs, and personal biases/beliefs/attitudes.

3. People high in need for achievement prefer moderate challenges, work well independently, and set personal goals. People high in need for affiliation prefer to work with others, enjoy the social aspects of a working environment, and often seek opportunities to please others. Those high in need for power want to influence or have an impact on others.

4. Some environmental factors that could affect the success of your presentation are climate, time of day, comfort level, and the size of your audience.

5. Some potential barriers to a successful presentation are political factors, financial factors, and personally offensive behavior.

Chapter 4

1. The hook (power opener), the line (the bulk of your content), and the sinker (powerful close) are the three essential elements of a presentation.

2. Some examples of hooks are a provocative question, a meaningful quote, an attractive visual, and an interesting statistic.

3. Capture the essence means to provide a brief overview of the entire presentation.

4. The three main ways of organizing the line of a presentation are topic, order, and position.

5. The three alternatives for providing order to the information in a presentation are alphabetical, continuum, and time.

6. A bridge statement provides a transition from the hook to the line and from the line to the sinker.

Chapter 5

1. The three major types of information elements for presentations are core, clarifying, and enriching information elements.

2. Some value-added dimensions to presentation information are quality, noise reduction, linkage, selectivity, precision, adaptability, flexibility, simplicity, ease of use, formatting, ordering, browsability, and time-saving.

3. The 4 Cs of presentation quality are correctness, completeness, currency, and credibility.

4. Content forms are visual, numerical, auditory, computer-based multimedia, and nonverbal information.

5. Some elements to consider when preparing the visual aspects of a presentation are the type of lettering, whether to use color and, if so, what colors, and whether to include static or moving images.

6. A table is appropriate when the presentation requires the display of raw data or for presenting several types of numerical information at once.

7. Some types of graphs and charts are bar graphs, line graphs, pie charts, and flow charts.

8. Information overload occurs when people are exposed to overwhelming amounts and type of information.

Chapter 6

1. Information literacy is the ability to find and collect desired information from a variety of sources and be able to locate, use, organize, synthesize, communicate, and evaluate that information.

2. Three well-known information problem-solving models are the Big6, the Research Process Model, and the Model of the Search Process.

3. What differentiates Kuhlthau's model from others is that it is based on several years of research in which she documented the process students use as they conduct their research activities.

4. Kuhlthau discovered that, rather than the research process being a neat, sequential set of skills, it is actually a learning process that is often quite messy and much more iterative (rather than linear) in nature.

5. The eight general research skills are definition, selection, planning, exploration, collection, organization, presentation, and evaluation.

Chapter 7

1. Some examples of written presentations that are intended for audiences internal to an organization are memos and job aids. Examples of written presentations that are intended for audiences external to an organization are business cards, business letters, and brochures. Examples of written presentations that can be either internal or external to an organization are resumes, handouts, abstracts, executive summaries, newsletters, and annual reports.

2. A job aid is an instructing presentation that helps a person remember learned information or processes to support work performance or other activities.

3. A cover letter is a business letter that explains an enclosure such as a resume or report.

4. Noise reduction is the most critical value-added factor for handouts.

5. An abstract provides an abbreviated representation of a larger presentation, reflecting its purpose and retaining its essential ideas in a brief format. Annotations are typically shorter than abstracts, contain less information, and may contain opinions regarding the document's usefulness or quality.

Chapter 8

1. Practice is the best way to relieve oral presentation anxiety. Some other methods are yawning, taking a deep breath, touching the floor, shrugging your shoulders, and shaking your body just before you present.

2. Ten traits that ensure that your presentation is a SUCCESS are a strong presence, the use of an effective hook and persuasive sinker, communication empathy with your audience, eye contact, enthusiasm, a satisfactory appearance, and sincerity.

3. Rate, volume, pitch, and articulation are four characteristics of your voice to consider when delivering an oral presentation.

4. The ARCS Model prescribes a number of motivational strategies to consider when developing a presentation.

5. Expectancy-value theory is the main theory underlying the ARCS Model.

6. The four ARCS components are attention, relevance, confidence, and satisfaction.

7. The ARCS component addressed by each of the following motivational strategies is:

a.	Incorporate humor.	Attention
b.	Provide extrinsic rewards.	Satisfaction
c.	Clarify expectations.	Confidence
d.	Ask a question.	Attention
e.	Match audience needs.	Relevance
f.	Actively listen.	Confidence
g.	Share experiences.	Relevance

8. Media can store and deliver information efficiently, help make abstract or complicated information simpler and more concrete, communicate and reinforce messages in forms that appeal to different cognitive styles, and are motivational by adding variety.

9. Body language such as certain gestures, smiling, nods, and eye contact can help to reinforce your message. Others like rattling your keys, stroking your beard, and clearing your throat can be distracting and detract from your message.

10. After your presentation, it is a good idea to take a few minutes and reflect on what went well and what could be improved for the next time.

Chapter 9

1. Text, audio, video, graphics, photographs, and animation are some types of media that can be combined in a multimedia presentation.

2. The uses of multimedia that pertain to presentations are:
- automated
- presenter-facilitated
- user-facilitated

3. Some upfront considerations that are important when planning multimedia presentations are establishing a budget, projecting a timeline, addressing legal concerns, conveying expectations, and deciding on whether or not to develop a prototype.

4. Repurposing refers to the re-use of existing materials such as graphics, video, animations, etc. in a new presentation. Repurposing helps the bottom line by eliminating the cost of original production.

5. It is important to acquire written copyright or legal permission when using outside sources of material for your multimedia presentation.

6. One of the most important functions of the project director is excellent communications with your project team including defining expectations.

7. A prototype is a sample of your project. It can be one fully developed piece or a mock-up of the entire project with limited functionality. The purpose of the prototype is to assist in decision-making by identifying needed changes before large expenditures are made.

8. Two additional dimensions of the content component of PACT that are associated with multimedia presentations are information design, which provides a logical structure for presenting information within a multimedia environment, and interface design, which includes the screen layout, menus, navigation aids, help systems, and everything that contributes to your audience's interactive experience.

9. Pre-production refers to all the planning and preparation that must be accomplished prior to actual production. Tasks include pre-interviewing on-camera subjects, location-scouting, developing a shooting plan, etc. Good pre-production saves valuable production time.

10. Alpha-testing is the first round of tests in a high-level multimedia project, usually conducted in-house to test functionality and correct any errors that are demonstrated. Beta-testing is conducted later, generally with members of the target audience who can provide feedback and identify any inconsistencies in the multimedia presentation.

Chapter 10

1. An evaluation determines the ability of your presentation to accomplish your purpose, meet the needs of your audience, and determine the quality of your content and the effectiveness of your technique.

2. The three types of evaluations are formative, summative, and follow-up evaluation.

3. Formative evaluation provides feedback data on the effectiveness of all aspects of presentation in order to revise it before it is delivered (or sometimes while it is in progress). Some methods for collecting formative data are focus groups, written feedback, discussions, one-on-one interviews, and videotaping.

4. The steps in conducting a focus group are:

- Gather a small group of three to five people who have characteristics similar to your target audience.
- Deliver the presentation as closely as possible to how the actual presentation will be presented.
- Ask participants to note their reactions, comments, and suggestions for improvement.
- Revise presentation where necessary.

5. Items for a survey or questionnaire may be designed as multiple choice questions or statements, checklists, Likert-type scales, and open-ended questions.

6. A rubric is a rating system by which presenters determine different, clearly-defined levels of performance effectiveness for each aspect of the presentation.

7. The steps for developing a rubric are:

- List the important aspects of the presentation.
- Define a limited number of performance criteria.
- Clearly and simply define performance criteria in terms of observable presentation behaviors or characteristics.

8. A follow-up evaluation is appropriate for gathering information to make further improvements or as additional evidence for future support.

9. The *WebMAC* is the *WebSite Motivational Analysis Checklist*, a set of instruments for evaluating Web resources. The *WebMAC* is based on expectancy-value theory.

10. Value and expectancy for success are *WebMAC*'s two evaluation components; stimulating, meaningful, organized, and easy-to-use are *WebMAC*'s four sub-components.

Appendix B

WebMAC Instruments

WebMAC E-Business©
Website Motivational Analysis Checklist
for Evaluating Service-Based Commercial Web Sites

DIRECTIONS:

Rate your level of agreement with each of the 32 items on the next two pages by placing the appropriate number value on the line in front of each item. If you are not sure about any item, select the best response you can give.

> **3** = strongly agree
> **2** = somewhat agree
> **1** = somewhat disagree
> **0** = strongly disagree
> **NA** = Not Applicable

Example of completed item:

<u>3</u> 0. This Web site is exciting.

After you have rated all 32 items, go back and look at each NA item. You should place one of the following scores next to the NA for that item.

0 = the Web site would have benefited if it had included the item (e.g., audio).
1 = the Web site didn't require that item.
2 = the Web site was better off for *not* including that item.

WebMAC E-Business©

Place the appropriate number about this Web site on the line preceding each item.

> 3 = strongly agree
> 2 = somewhat agree
> 1 = somewhat disagree
> 0 = strongly disagree
> NA = Not Applicable

_____ 1. The home page of this Web site is eye-catching and visually interesting.

_____ 2. The information at this Web site is accurate and unbiased (or the bias is properly identified).

_____ 3. Any visuals (e.g., videos, photographs) or audio included in this Web site enhance the presentation of service(s) and information offered.

_____ 4. The screen layout makes the site easy to navigate.

_____ 5. There are incentives at this site that motivate me to explore it.

_____ 6. This Web site provides links to other relevant Web sites.

_____ 7. This Web site provides enough information about the services offered.

_____ 8. The Web site has a help function that I can use at any time.

_____ 9. The screen layout of this Web site is attractive.

_____ 10. This Web site provides information that allows me to judge the company's credibility.

_____ 11. There is a menu or site map that helps me understand how this Web site is organized.

_____ 12. I can control how fast I move through this Web site at all times.

_____ 13. The information at this Web site is written in an interesting manner.

_____ 14. The information at this Web site appears to be current and up-to-date.

_____ 15. The purpose of this Web site is always clear to me.

_____ 16. Navigating this Web site does not require any special skills or experience.

_____ 17. The variety of formats for presenting information (e.g., text, images, sound) keeps my attention.

_____ 18. This Web site has clear and complete information about service fees and other charges.

_____ 19. All of the information at this Web site is presented using clear and consistent language and style, without grammatical or spelling errors.

_____ 20. All of this Web site's links are active and fully functioning.

_____ 21. This Web site has novel or unique features that make it more engaging.

_____ 22. This Web site allows opportunities to communicate with the company.

_____ 23. Adequate information is provided to indicate this company will deliver timely service and customer support.

_____ 24. At all times, I can control what information at this Web site I wish to see.

_____ 25. The colors and/or background patterns used in this Web site are pleasing.

_____ 26. This Web site provides opportunities for interactivity.

_____ 27. The directions for using this Web site are simple and clear.

_____ 28. All buttons and other navigation mechanisms for moving around at this Web site work the way they should.

_____ 29. The music and/or sound effects used at this site are pleasing without being distracting.

_____ 30. There is little or no unimportant or redundant information at this Web site.

_____ 31. No matter where I am in this Web site, I can return to the home page or exit.

_____ 32. The amount of time it takes for pictures, games, videos, etc. to appear on the screen at this Web site is reasonable.

- -

I would consider re-visiting this Web site in the future.
YES ☐   NO ☐
I would recommend this Web site to others.
YES ☐   NO ☐

What is the greatest strength of this Web site?

What needs improvement at this Web site?

WebMAC E-Business©

Scoring *WebMAC E-Business*

Before transferring scores, go back to each item designated as "NA" and choose a score for that item based on the following criteria:

      0 points if you feel that the site would have benefited if it had included the item (e.g., audio).

      1 point if you feel that the Web site didn't require that item.

      2 points if you believe the site was better off for *not* including that item.

When all 32 items have a number score, transfer each score into the appropriately numbered space in one of the four columns below. Circle all items with a score of 0 or 1 as those that you may want to specifically address later. Now add all the scores for each column and write the total on the appropriate line.

S	M	O	E
1. ___	2. ___	3. ___	4. ___
5. ___	6. ___	7. ___	8. ___
9. ___	10. ___	11. ___	12. ___
13. ___	14. ___	15. ___	16. ___
17. ___	18. ___	19. ___	20. ___
21. ___	22. ___	23. ___	24. ___
25. ___	26. ___	27. ___	28. ___
29. ___	30. ___	31. ___	32. ___
TOTAL S ___	TOTAL M ___	TOTAL O ___	TOTAL E ___

The **S** column reflects how STIMULATING this Web site is for you.
The **M** column reflects how MEANINGFUL this Web site is to you.
The **O** column reflects how ORGANIZED you think this Web site is.
The **E** column reflects how EASY TO USE this Web site is for you.

WebMAC E-Business⁰

Transforming Scores

Now you may transform your scores into visual representations so that you can clearly see the results of your evaluation.

1. Take each of the four total scores above and plot them (either with a dot or a bar) on the graph below.

2. If you use dots, connect the dots to make a line.

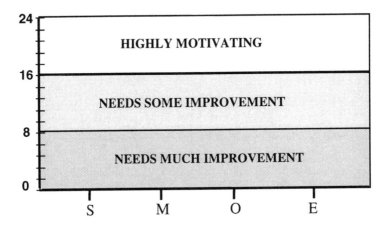

Now take the total scores from the four categories (S, M, O, E) and add them together in the following way to get your two overall motivational quality scores.

$$S + M = \text{_____} \ (V) \qquad\qquad O + E = \text{_____} \ (XS)$$

The **V** score reflects a summary motivation score on the Value dimension; i.e., how stimulating and meaningful the Web site is. The **XS** score reflects a summary motivation score on the Expectation for Success dimension; i.e., how organized and easy to use the Web site is.

WebMAC E-Business©

Plotting the Scores

To plot scores on the scoring grid,

1. Place a dot for the **V** score along the Value continuum and a dot for the **XS** score along the Expectation for Success continuum on the grid.

2. Draw straight lines to their intersection point, representing the overall motivational quality score of the Web site.

In the example below the evaluated Web site received a Value score of 40 and an Expectation for Success score of 18. Their intersection point falls within the lower right quadrant of the grid.

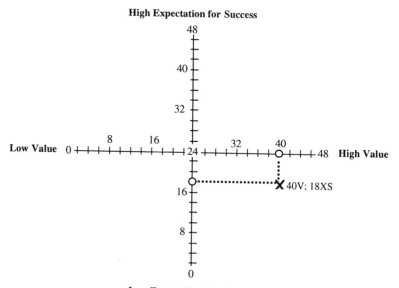

WebMAC E-Business©

Recording Actual Scores

To record your actual scores onto the scoring grid.

1. Plot the score for **V** along the Value continuum and the score for **XS** along the Expectation for Success continuum.

2. Draw straight lines to the intersection point.

3. A score in the uppermost part of the upper right hand section makes this site an Awesome Web Site.

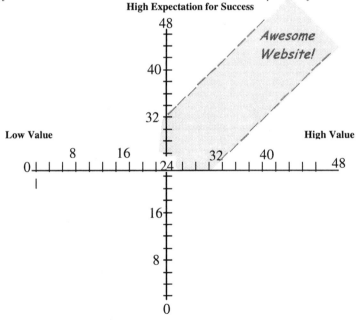

Average to high for expectation for success/Below average to low for value

Average to high for value/ Average to high for expectation for success

High Expectation for Success

Awesome Website!

Low Value   **High Value**

Below average to low for value/ Below average to low for expectation for success

Average to high for value/ Below average to low for expectation for success

Low Expectation for Success

WebMAC E-Commerce©
Website Motivational Analysis Checklist
For Evaluating Product-Based Commercial Web Sites

DIRECTIONS:

Rate your level of agreement with each of the 32 items on the next two pages by placing the appropriate number value on the line in front of each item. If you are not sure about any item, select the best response you can give.

3 = strongly agree
2 = somewhat agree
1 = somewhat disagree
0 = strongly disagree
NA = Not Applicable

Example of completed item:

3 0. This Web site is exciting.

After you have rated all 32 items, go back and look at each NA item. You should place one of the following scores next to the NA for that item.

0 = the Web site would have benefited if it had included the item (e.g., audio).
1 = the Web site didn't require that item.
2 = the Web site was better off for *not* including that item.

WebMAC E-Commerce©

Place the appropriate number about this Web site on the line preceding each item.

>3 = strongly agree
>2 = somewhat agree
>1 = somewhat disagree
>0 = strongly disagree
>NA = Not Applicable

_____ 1. The home page of this Web site is eye-catching and visually interesting.

_____ 2. This Web site provides clear and complete product ordering and pricing information.

_____ 3. Any visual (e.g., video, photograph, animation) or audio information included in this Web site enhances product presentation.

_____ 4. I can control how fast I move through this Web site at all times.

_____ 5. The screen layout of this Web site is attractive.

_____ 6. This Web site provides links to other relevant Web sites.

_____ 7. This Web site provides enough information about the product(s) offered.

_____ 8. The Web site has a <u>help</u> function that I can use at any time.

_____ 9. There are incentives at this site that motivate me to explore it.

_____ 10. This Web site provides information that allows me to judge the company's credibility.

_____ 11. There is a menu or site map that helps me understand how this Web site is organized.

_____ 12. The amount of time it takes for pictures, games, videos, etc. to appear on the screen at this Web site is reasonable.

_____ 13. The variety of formats for presenting information (e.g., text, images, sound) keeps my attention.

_____ 14. The information presented at this Web site appears to be current and up-to-date.

_____ 15. Text information is broken up into readable segments.

_____ 16. Navigating this Web site does not require any special skills or experience.

_____ 17. Product information at this Web site is written in an interesting manner.

_____ 18. All product information appears to be represented accurately.

WebMAC E-Commerce©

___ 19. All of the information at this Web site is presented using clear and consistent language and style, without grammatical or spelling errors.

___ 20. All of this Web site's links are active and fully functioning.

___ 21. This Web site has novel or unique features that make it more interesting.

___ 22. This Web site allows opportunities to communicate with the company (e.g., customer service).

___ 23. Adequate information is provided to indicate this company provides timely product delivery and customer support.

___ 24. At all times, I can control what information at this Web site I wish to see.

___ 25. The colors and/or background patterns used in this Web site are pleasing.

___ 26. This Web site provides opportunities for interactivity.

___ 27. The directions for using this Web site are simple and clear.

___ 28. All buttons and other navigation mechanisms for moving around at this Web site work the way they should.

___ 29. The music and/or sound effects used at this site are pleasing without being distracting.

___ 30. There is an effort at this Web site to inform me of the company's policy on customer privacy.

___ 31. No matter where I am in this Web site, I can return to the home page or exit.

___ 32. The ordering process at this site is reasonable in terms of speed and convenience.

- -

I would consider re-visiting this Web site in the future.
YES ☐   NO ☐
I would recommend this Web site to others.
YES ☐   NO ☐

What is the greatest strength of this Web site?

What needs improvement at this Web site?

WebMAC E-Commerce®

Scoring *WebMAC E-Commerce*

Before transferring scores, go back to each item designated as "NA" and choose a score for that item based on the following criteria:

- 0 points if you feel that the site would have benefited if it had included the item (e.g. audio).
- 1 point if you feel that the Web site didn't require that item.
- 2 points if you believe the site was better off for *not* including that item.

When all 32 items have a number score, transfer each score into the appropriately numbered space in one of the four columns below. Circle all items with a score of 0 or 1 as those that you may want to specifically address later. Now add all the scores for each column and write the total on the appropriate line.

<u>S</u>	<u>M</u>	<u>O</u>	<u>E</u>
1. ___	2. ___	3. ___	4. ___
5. ___	6. ___	7. ___	8. ___
9. ___	10. ___	11. ___	12. ___
13. ___	14. ___	15. ___	16. ___
17. ___	18. ___	19. ___	20. ___
21. ___	22. ___	23. ___	24. ___
25. ___	26. ___	27. ___	28. ___
29. ___	30. ___	31. ___	32. ___
TOTAL S ___	TOTAL M ___	TOTAL O ___	TOTAL E ___

The **S** column reflects how STIMULATING this Web site is for you.
The **M** column reflects how MEANINGFUL this Web site is to you.
The **O** column reflects how ORGANIZED you think this Web site is.
The **E** column reflects how EASY TO USE this Web site is for you.

WebMAC E-Commerce©

Transforming Scores

Now you may transform your scores into visual representations so that you can clearly see the results of your evaluation.

1. Take each of the four total scores above and plot them (either with a dot or a bar) on the graph below.

2. If you use dots, connect the dots to make a line.

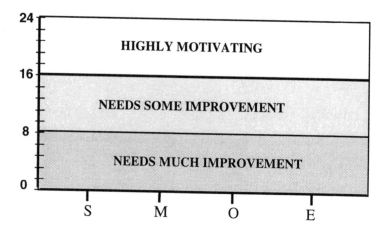

Now take the total scores from the four categories (S, M, O, E) and add them together in the following way to get your two overall motivational quality scores.

$$S + M = \text{_____} \text{ (V)} \qquad\qquad O + E = \text{_____} \text{ (XS)}$$

The **V** score reflects a summary motivation score on the Value dimension; i.e., how stimulating and meaningful the Web site is. The **XS** score reflects a summary motivation score on the Expectation for Success dimension; i.e., how organized and easy to use the Web site is.

WebMAC E-Commerce©

Plotting the Scores

To plot scores on the scoring grid,

1. Place a dot for the **V** score along the Value continuum and a dot for the **XS** score along the Expectation for Success continuum on the grid.

2. Draw straight lines to their intersection point, representing the overall motivational quality score of the Web site.

In the example below, the evaluated Web site received a Value score of 40 and an Expectation for Success score of 18. Their intersection point falls within the lower right quadrant of the grid.

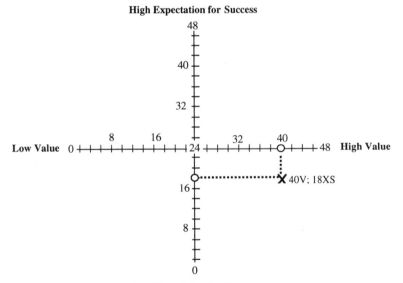

WebMAC E-Commerce©

Recording Actual Scores

To record your actual scores onto the scoring grid.

1. Plot the score for **V** along the Value continuum and the score for **XS** along the Expectation for Success continuum.

2. Draw straight lines to the intersection point.

3. A score in the uppermost part of the upper right hand section makes this site an Awesome Web Site.

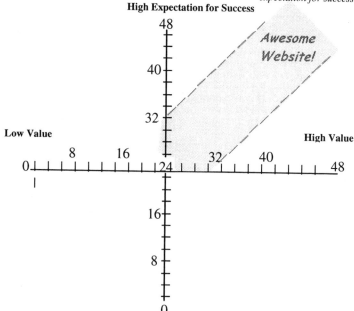

Average to high for expectation for success/Below average to low for value

Average to high for value/ Average to high for expectation for success

High Expectation for Success

Awesome Website!

Low Value

High Value

Low Expectation for Success

Below average to low for value/ Below average to low for expectation for success

Average to high for value/ Below average to low for expectation for success

Bibliography

American Association of School Librarians and Association for Educational Communications and Technology. *Information Power: Building Partnerships for Learning.* Chicago: American Library Association, 1998.

Arnone, Marilyn P., and Ruth V. Small. *Website Motivational Analysis Checklist for Electronic Business (WebMAC E-Business).* Fayetteville, N.Y.: The Motivation Mining Company, 2000.

Ayers, J.B. *Evaluating Workshops and Institutes,* ERIC Digest. Washington, D.C.: American Institutes for Research, 1989. (ED315427)

Caplinger, Cory. *Myers-Briggs Introduction,* Aug. 3, 2000. (http://www.geocities.com/ lifexplore/)

Clarke, Steven, and B. Lehaney, eds. *Human Centered Methods in Information Systems: Current Research and Practice.* Hershey, Pa.: Idea Group Publishing, 2000.

Cremmins, Edward T. *The Art of Abstracting.* Washington, D.C.: Educational Resources Information Center, U.S. Department of Education, 1982. (ED224496)

D'Arcy, Jan. *Technically Speaking: Proven Ways to Make Your Next Presentation a Success.* New York: American Management Association, 1992.

Eisenberg, Michael B., and Robert Berkowitz. *Information Problem Solving: The Big Six Skills Approach to Library and Information Skills Instruction,* Norwood, N.J.: Ablex, 1990.

ERIC Processing Manual, Section V: Cataloging. Washington, D.C.: Educational Resources Information Center, U.S. Department of Education, June 1992, V13-16.

Fielden, John. "What Do You Mean I Can't Write?" *Harvard Business Review.* (May/June 1964).

Geis, George L. "Formative Evaluation: Developmental Testing and Expert Review." *Performance & Instruction* (May/June 1987), 1-8.

Hall, Edward T. *The Silent Language.* Greenwich, Conn.: Fawcett Publications, 1959.

Howles, L., and Pettengill, C. "Designing Instructional Multimedia Presentations: A Seven-Step Process." *T.H.E. Journal* (June 1993), 58-61.

Jackson, Tom, and Ellen Jackson. *The New Perfect Resume Breakthrough Resumes for Today's Best Careers.* New York: Doubleday, 1996.

240   Bibliography

Karlins, Marvin, and Herbert I. Abelson. *Persuasion: How Opinions and Attitudes are Changed*. New York: Springer Publishing, 1970.

Keller, John M. "Strategies for Stimulating the Motivation to Learn." *Performance & Instruction* (Oct. 1987), 1-7.

Kuhlthau, Carol. "Implementing a Process Approach to Information Skills: A Study Identifying Indicators of Success in Library Media Programs." *School Library Media Quarterly* 22, no. 1 (1993): 11-18.

————. "Inside the Search Process: Information Seeking from the User's Perspective." *Journal of the American Society of Information Science* 42, no. 5 (1991): 361-371.

Lambert, Clark. *The Business Presentations Workbook*. Englewood Cliffs, N.J.: Prentice-Hall, 1989.

Mandel, Steve. *Effective Presentation Skills: A Practical Guide for Better Speaking*. Rev. ed. Menlo Park, Calif.: Crisp Publications, Inc., 1993.

Martinetz, Charles F. "How to Make Instructional Presentations." *Performance & Instruction* (March 1988), 6-8.

McClelland, David C. *Human Motivation*. Cambridge: Cambridge University Press, 1998.

Molloy, John T. *Dress for Success*. New York: Warner Books, 1976.

Motley, Michael. "Taking the Terror Out of Talk." *Psychology Today* (Jan. 1988), 46-48.

Myers, Isabel Briggs, and Mary McCaulley. *Manual: A Guide to the Development and Use of the Myers-Briggs Type Indicator*. Palo Alto, Calif.: Consulting Psychologist Press, 1985.

Naisbitt, John, and Patricia Aburdene. *Megatrends 2000*. New York: William Morrow & Company, Inc., 1990.

Nielsen, Jakob. "Heuristic Evaluation." In *Usability Inspection Methods*, edited by J. Nielsen and R.L. Mack. New York: John Wiley & Sons, 1994.

Peoples, David. *Presentations Plus*, 2nd ed. New York: John Wiley & Sons, 1992.

Raines, Claire. *Visual Aids in Business: A Guide for Effective Presentations*. Menlo Park, Calif.: Crisp Publications, Inc., 1989.

Rossett, Allison, and Jeannette Gautier-Downes. *A Handbook of Job Aids*. San Francisco, Calif.: Pfeiffer, 1991.

Rowe, Mary Budd. "Wait Time: Slowing Down May Be a Way of Speeding Up!" *Journal of Teacher Education* 37, no. 1 (January-February 1986): 43-50.

Saffo, Paul. "Managing Information—Infoglut: New Tools Can Help Tame an Ocean of Data." *Information Week* (Oct. 30, 1995).

Shneiderman, Ben. *Designing the User Interface: Strategies for Effective Human-Computer Interaction*, 2nd ed. Reading, Mass.: Addison-Wesley Publishing Company, Inc., 1993.

Simmons, Silvia. *How to Be the Life of the Podium*. New York: American Management Association, 1991.

Small, Ruth V. "Having an IM-PACT on Information Literacy." *Teacher-Librarian: The Journal for School Library Professionals*, 28, no. 1 (Oct. 2000): 30-35.

―――. *Turning Kids On to Research: The Power of Motivation*, Englewood: Colo.: Libraries Unlimited, 2000.

Website Motivational Analysis Checklist for Electronic Commerce (WebMAC E-Commerce). Fayetteville, N.Y.: The Motivation Mining Company, 2000.

Staley, Hank. *Tongue & Quill*. Washington, D.C.: Pergamon-Brassey's International Defense Publishers, Inc., 1990.

Stripling, Barbara, and Judy Pitts. *Brainstorms and Blueprints: Teaching Library Research As a Thinking Process*. Englewood, Colo.: Libraries Unlimited, 1988.

Taylor, Robert S. *Value-Added Processes in Information Systems*. Norwood, N.J.: Ablex, 1986.

Tufte, Edward R. *The Visual Display of Quantitative Information*. Cheshire, Conn.: Graphics Press, 1983.

Vroom, Victor H. *Work and Motivation*. New York: Wiley, 1964.

Weaver, Richard L. *Understanding Interpersonal Communication*, 4th ed. Glenview, Ill.: Scott, Foresman, 1987.

Wurman, Richard Saul. *Information Anxiety*. New York: Bantam Books, 1989.

About the Authors

Ruth V. Small, Ph.D., is professor of Information Studies (IST) at Syracuse University and has served as director of its school media program since 1991. Dr. Small received a Master's degree in Library Science from Syracuse University, a Master's degree in Education from Hunter College, and a doctorate in Instructional Design, Development and Evaluation from Syracuse University. Ruth's research focuses on the motivational aspects of information use; her work earned her the 2001 Carroll Preston Baber Research Award from the American Library Association and the 1997 Highsmith Research Award from the American Association of School Librarians. She has more than seventy publications to her credit, including five books, and has delivered hundreds of formal and informal presentations around the world. Ruth has served as a design and evaluation consultant to a wide variety of organizations, such as the University of Sao Paulo (Brazil), the Dewitt Wallace-Readers Digest Fund, the U.S. Department of Education, and Switzerland's International Institute for Management Development. In 1996, she was recognized for outstanding teaching performance with her school's "Professor of the Year" award.

Marilyn P. Arnone, Ph.D., is president, Research and Development, and co-founder of Creative Media Solutions, Inc. (CMS) in Syracuse, New York, and Philadelphia, a full service video and multimedia production company serving both regional and national clients. Dr. Arnone has a special interest in children's media and has worked in various roles including creator, consultant, producer, instructional designer, and director of evaluation on numerous video, multimedia, and broadcast projects, such as The Learning Channel's (TLC) *Pappyland*, the syndicated life-skill oriented television vignette series *Kidsminute*, and *Young Researchers*, a series of videos designed to foster information literacy skills featuring real kids. Her research interests center on exploring children's curiosity and learning in interactive learning environments. She has published in leading journals in her field, written four books with co-author Dr. Ruth Small and presented at conferences nationwide. Marilyn received her B.S. degree from Emerson College with a communications concentration, her master's degree in Education from Harvard University Graduate School of Education and earned her doctorate from Syracuse University School of Education in Instructional Design, Development, and Evaluation. Marilyn is assistant adjunct professor at Syracuse University's School of Information Studies.